Literacy in Action

Authors

Dr. Sharon Jeroski

Andrea Bishop
Jean Bowman
Lynn Bryan
Linda Charko
Maureen Dockendorf
Christine Finochio
Jo Ann Grime
Joanne Leblanc-Haley
Deidre McConnell
Carol Munro
Cathie Peters
Lorraine Prokopchuk
Arnold Toutant

PEARSON

Education
Canada

Grade 4 Project Team

Team Leader: Anita Borovilos
National Literacy Consultant: Norma MacFarlane
Publisher: Susan Green
Product Manager: Donna Neumann
Managing Editor: Gaynor Fitzpatrick
Sr. Developmental Editor: Anne MacInnes
Editor: Kathleen ffolliott
Production/Copy Editor: Jessica Westhead
Production Coordinator: Zane Kaneps
Art Director: Zena Denchik
Designers: Zena Denchik and Anthony Leung
Permissions Research: Cindy Howard
Photo Research: Christina Beamish, Cindy Howard, and
Mary Rose MacLachlan
Vice-President Publishing and Marketing: Mark Cobham

ISBN 0-13-204701-2 (softcover)
ISBN 0-13-204700-4 (hardcover)

Printed and bound in Canada.
 2 3 4 5   TC   10 09 08 07

The publisher has taken every care to meet or exceed industry
specifications for the manufacturing of textbooks. The cover of this sewn
book is a premium, polymer-reinforced material designed to provide long life
and withstand rugged use. Mylar gloss lamination has been applied for
further durability.

Acknowledgements

Series Consultants

Andrea Bishop
Anne Boyd
Christine Finochio
Joanne Leblanc-Haley

Don Jones
Jill Maar
Joanne Rowlandson
Carole Stickley

Specialist Reviewers

Science: Doug Herridge
    Toronto, ON
Social Studies: Marg Lysecki
    Toronto, ON
Aboriginal: Ken Ealey
    Edmonton, AB

Equity: Dianna Mezzarobba
    Vancouver, BC
Levelling: Iris Zammit
    Toronto, ON

Grades 3–6 Advisors and Reviewers

Dr. Frank Serafini
    Assistant Professor,
    University of Las Vegas,
    Las Vegas, Nevada

Patricia Adamson
    Winnipeg, MB
Marion Ahrens
    Richmond Hill, ON
Sandra Ball
    Surrey, BC
Gwen Bartnik
    Vancouver, BC
Jennifer Batycky
    Calgary, AB
Michelle Bellavia
    Hamilton, ON
Mary-Jane Black
    Hamilton, ON
Jackie Bradley
    Saskatoon, SK
Diane Campbell
    Durham, ON
Nancy Carl
    Coquitlam, BC
Janet Chow
    Burnaby, BC
Marla Ciccotelli
    London, ON
Susan Clarke
    Burlington, ON
Norma Collinson
    Truro, NS
Lynn Crews
    Lower Sackville, NS

Kathryn D'Angelo
    Richmond, BC
Susan Elliott
    Toronto, ON
Diane Gagley
    Calgary, AB
Michael Gallant
    Calgary, AB
Jennifer Gardner
    Vernon, BC
Adrienne Gear
    Vancouver, BC
Faye Gertz
    Niska, AB
Cindy Gordon
    Victoria, BC
James Gray
    Winnipeg, MB
Kathleen Gregory
    Victoria, BC
Myrtis Guy
    Torbay, NL
Kim Guyette-Carter
    Dartmouth, NS
Jackie Hall
    Vancouver, BC
Natalie Harnum
    Berwick, NS
Deborah Holley
    Duncan, BC
Joanne Holme
    Surrey, BC
Patricia Horstead
    Maple Ridge, BC
Carol Hryniuk-Adamov
    Winnipeg, MB

Pamela Jacob
    Limestone, ON
Joanne Keller
    Delta, BC
Dawn Kesslering
    Regina, SK
Karen Quan King
    Toronto, ON
Linda Kirby
    Sault Ste. Marie, ON
Sheryl Koers
    Duncan, BC
Roger Lacey
    Calgary, AB
Caroline Lutyk
    Burlington, ON
Heather MacKay
    Richmond, BC
Margaret Marion
    Niagara Falls, ON
Sangeeta McAuley
    Toronto, ON
Paula McIntee
    Allanburg, ON
Caroline Mitchell
    Guelph, ON
Laura Mossey
    Durham, ON
Rhonda Nixon
    Edmonton, AB
Gillian Parsons
    Brantford, ON
Linda Perrin
    Saint John, NB
Charolette Player
    Edmonton, AB

Rhonda Rakimov
    Duncan, BC
Tammy Renyard
    Duncan, BC
Kristine Richards
    Windsor, ON
Kathryn Richmond
    St. Catharines, ON
Barbara Rushton
    New Minas, NS
Jaye Sawatsky
    Delta, BC
Michelle Sharratt
    Woodbridge, ON
Cathy Sheridan
    Ottawa, ON
Nanci-Jane Simpson
    Hamilton, ON
Kim Smith
    Newmarket, ON
Candace Spilsbury
    Duncan, BC
Patricia Tapp
    Hamilton, ON
Vera Teschow
    Mississauga, ON
Joanne Traczuk
    Sutton West, ON
Sonja Willier
    Edmonton, AB
Susan Wilson
    St. Catharines, ON
Kelly Winney
    London, ON
Beth Zimmerman
    London, ON

CONTENTS

UNIT 4

What Are Your Hobbies? • 2

Read Together

Shared

Learn Together Poster

Guided Practice

Literacy in Action

Independent Practice

Read! Write! Say! Do!

Your Literacy Portfolio

Make Me Laugh! • 62

Read Together

Shared

Learn Together Poster

Guided Practice

Literacy in Action

Independent Practice

Read! Write! Say! Do!

Your Literacy Portfolio

UNIT 6

Amazing Places! • 120

Read Together

Shared

Learn Together Poster

Guided Practice

Literacy in Action

Independent Practice

Read! Write! Say! Do!

Your Literacy Portfolio

What Are **Your** Hobbies?

LEARNING GOALS

In this unit you will:

- Read and view news articles about interesting activities and hobbies.

- Combine and compare information from different sources.

- Ask questions and listen actively to gather new information.

- Write and present newspaper articles.

hobbies
leisure activities
skills
collecting
just for fun
record holders

3

What I Did with My Coin Collection

by Tiger Woods
Illustrated by Sarah S. Brannen

How did Tiger Woods use his hobby to help others?

When I was about five, maybe six, years old, I loved to collect coins. I had about a dozen of them, and most special of all were the gold coins—each one big and shiny and sparkling like the sun. My favourite was a twenty-dollar Canadian gold piece.

But if I loved anything in the world more than my coins, it was my own set of golf clubs. My father had made them especially for me. (He took regular grown-up clubs and cut them down to my size.) I kept my clubs in the garage, where Dad had built a big net so I could hit the ball as hard as I wanted to—right into it. He also put in a special green carpet, where I could practise putting.

4

One night I was watching the news with my father. The man on TV was Walter Cronkite, and he was telling a story about families who lived in Ethiopia, a country in the eastern part of Africa. Their lives were terrible, said Mr. Cronkite. Men and women and boys and girls there were starving to death. Really starving. They had no food at all.

I stared at the TV, more frightened than I'd ever been. The faces of these children were so sad, and flies buzzed around their heads. But it was their eyes that were the scariest of all—big and wide-open and terrified.

I had never even imagined that kids could be this unhappy. I was their age, and I lived in a nice house in California. I had my own room, with my own little TV set. I had a tricycle. I was going to school. And all these kids wanted was just a crust of bread, maybe.

My father saw the look on my face and said, "You know, Tiger, I have a doctor friend who is over in Africa right now, working to help these children."

"That's good," I said, not really feeling much better.

Then my dad quietly explained to me how lucky I was to be living a good and healthy life. He told me that it wasn't the fault of these Ethiopian children that they were starving. He said people all over the world were trying to send food and help to them.

As I listened to my father, I never took my eyes off the TV. Then I got up and went to my room. I stood in the doorway and looked around.

There was my little television. There were my books and my toys. There was my favourite golf club, lying across my bed. And there were my precious coins, the gold Canadian one right on top. The strange thing was, as I looked at all my wonderful stuff, I got very, very sad inside. I kept seeing the faces of those Ethiopian kids. Suddenly the world didn't seem very fair to me, and I knew what I had to do.

I went back to the living room with my box of coins. I gave them to my father, who was still watching TV.

"Daddy," I said, "would you send these to your friend in Africa so he can help those kids and buy some food for them?"

"Are you sure, Tiger?" he asked me. "I know how much you love them."

"I'm sure, Daddy."

My father gave me a hug and said, "Yes, Tiger, I will send them to Africa for you." He took the box of coins from me, and that was that.

For as long as I can remember, we've had a special family saying: "Share and care." Dad tells me that the first time he said those words to me was the day I was born. I don't remember that day, of course, but he and my mother never let a day go by without telling me that we must remember to help others. *Share and care*. I still say those words to myself every day.

By the way, a lot of good things in my life came from those coins. Because I was so interested in Africa as a little boy, I wound up playing golf there when I got older, at a tournament to raise money for people who needed help. And it's also where I got to meet the great leader of South Africa, Nelson Mandela, who helped gain freedom for his people.

Did I ever miss my coins? Sometimes—but that's okay. Because one thing I've learned is that, in the end, sharing and caring is worth a million pieces of gold.

LET'S TALK ABOUT IT...

- How did Tiger Woods use his coin collection to show that he was "sharing and caring"?

- Tiger Woods collected coins. What other kinds of collections do you know about? Why do you think people enjoy collecting things?

Nelson Mandela (middle) with Tiger and his dad. Nelson Mandela won the Nobel Peace Prize in 1993.

Read News Articles

Newspapers, magazines, and Web sites have articles about real people and events. Radio and television stations broadcast news stories about people and events too.

Think about a story you have read, heard, or viewed about an interesting person or activity.

TALK ABOUT IT!

- Share your story with a partner or a group.
- Tell what the story was about and what made it interesting.

Here are places you can find news articles or stories.

CBC Radio-Canada

Together, make a list of interesting articles you have found.

News Articles

What article was about	Where I read or saw it

Think Like a Reader

Read and view with a purpose

- Why do you read articles about people?

Crack the code

Reporters often include quotes from people to add interest. Quotation marks show the exact words that were spoken. What do you notice about the punctuation in this example?

> My father gave me a hug and said, **"Yes, Tiger, I will send them to Africa for you."**

Make meaning

Practise using these strategies when you read articles:

USE WHAT YOU KNOW — Before you read, look at the title and pictures to find out the topic. Then ask yourself: What do I already know about this topic?

VISUALIZE — Use the information to make a picture in your mind.

SYNTHESIZE — Put ideas together. How does information fit with other information you have read or viewed?

Analyze what you read

- How do the pictures with an article affect how you feel about the subject?
- Articles sometimes quote certain people. How might an article change depending on who is quoted in it?

A rock and roll summer

by Cathy Fraccaro
Staff Reporter

Imagine going to school in the summer. Nine-year-old Issabella DiPoce did. She went to a school of rock and roll!

Issabella is in Grade 4 and loves to play the drums. She and her brother spent a week at the School of Rock 'N' Roll Summer Camp. It was at Durham College in Oshawa, Ontario. This camp is for boys and girls from nine to sixteen.

How did Issabella get started on drums? "I've been playing drums for over a year," she says. "My uncle plays the drums and he's my teacher. We have a drum kit, a piano, and a keyboard at home. My brother has a guitar."

Issabella's mother found the School of Rock 'N' Roll on the Internet. She knew her kids would love it. They would have a chance to let loose and create some of their own music. The counsellors would help them improve their music skills.

Although Issabella was the youngest camper, she was not at all scared. "We all learned how to play in a band, write songs, and use the proper stage equipment," she says. "One counsellor helped me with drum

Issabella DiPoce

lessons. At the end of camp, we had a Festival of Rock. We performed for our families and friends on stage. I played the drums in our group."

She adds, "Some people are surprised that I play the drums because I'm a girl and I'm very young. Playing the drums makes me so happy."

When she is in Grade 7, Issabella will be able to play in her school band. Until then, she'll go to summer school—the School of Rock 'N' Roll, that is!

VISUALIZE
Imagine what the campers' music sounded like.

Campers perform for family and friends at the Festival of Rock.

SYNTHESIZE
How is this camp like other camps you know about? How is it different?

DAILY

You don't have to run away to join the circus!

USE WHAT YOU KNOW

What do you know about circus performers?

by Cathy Fraccaro
Staff Reporter

Ten-year-old Hilton Eang learned this when he and his brother went to a Circus Arts camp. It was offered by CirKids in Vancouver.

Hilton explains, "My mom had often seen the CirKids ad in the newspaper. She asked if we would like to try it. I had never taken gymnastics or tried to juggle. I couldn't even ride a bicycle!"

Hilton's mother had learned that the camp was for kids from seven to fourteen. They went for a week. They could learn circus skills, like juggling and walking on the tight wire. They could try the trapeze, the mini-trampoline, and more. Dance, theatre, and athletics were part of the CirKids program too.

When asked what he did at the camp, Hilton's eyes light up. "First I learned how to warm up my muscles with stretching exercises. Then I tried juggling, balancing on a large ball, and hanging from a trapeze. I rode a unicycle, built 'people pyramids,' and bounced on a trampoline. I even walked on the tight wire—low at first and then higher each time. Our coaches were great! On the last day, we dressed in costume and performed for our families."

Hilton Eang

12

NEWS

VISUALIZE

Imagine performing circus acts. Create a picture in your mind.

The Eang boys had a great time at the camp. Now both have signed up for the regular programs. "I spend four hours every Sunday at CirKids," says Hilton. "My circus skills have really improved. I can juggle three balls. I can ride a unicycle for 8 metres without falling. In tumbling, I can do six front rolls in a row. I used to get dizzy from doing just one!"

Hilton adds, "I really hope I can go back to the camp next summer."

Young CirKids performers show what they've learned.

SYNTHESIZE

How is this camp like other camps you know about? How is it different?

13

DAILY

Young fossil hunter attends a "dino-mite" camp

by Cathy Fraccaro
Staff Reporter

Ten-year-old Jade Pryor read a pamphlet about the Royal Tyrrell Museum's Junior Adventure Camp in Drumheller, Alberta. It was a five-day overnight camp for boys and girls from nine to eleven. She knew this was the right summer camp for her.

Jade Pryor

"I've been interested in fossils and dinosaurs forever," says Jade. "I always go out and collect rocks and things. My bedroom is full of rocks and fossils."

Trained counsellors help the campers as they search for fossils and make dinosaur casts. The campers sleep in teepees. There are other teepees for cooking, eating, and playing games.

What was a day at camp like? "Every day we would walk to the museum to fill our water bottles," Jade says. "Then we would hike to different activity sites. We went digging with proper tools like the ones scientists use. We cleaned the fossils we found. Some days we explored the

14

NEWS

VISUALIZE

Imagine searching and digging for fossils. Create a picture in your mind.

museum. And I got to make a cast of a dinosaur tooth!"

Asked what part of camp she enjoyed the most, Jade replies, "It was great fun digging for dinosaurs. And I liked the camp theme. It was about an evil doctor who was trying to get rid of all the fossils in the world."

And what did she learn? "I learned if dinosaur bones are found all facing the same way, then you know the dinosaur died in a river. The current had moved the bones into line. And scientists once thought that dinosaurs walked with their tails curled. Then they found out that when dinosaurs die, the tendons in their tails tighten up. This makes the tails look like they had been curled."

When asked if she would go again, Jade replies, "Oh, yes! When I'm twelve, I want to go to the Senior Science Finders Camp. Then I'll get to canoe on the Red Deer River to look for fossils."

Campers inspect dinosaur bones in the museum.

SYNTHESIZE

How is this camp like other camps you know about? How is it different?

15

Two campers carefully dig for fossils.

Reflect on Your Reading

You have ...

- talked about hobbies and interests you and others enjoy.
- practised picking out the exact words of a speaker.
- read articles about interesting people and their activities.

> I'm learning to play the drums. I practise every chance I get.

> When I read an article, I look for quotation marks to see exactly what someone said.

You have also ...

- explored different reading strategies.

USE WHAT YOU KNOW

VISUALIZE

SYNTHESIZE

Write About Learning

Write about one of the strategies you used when you read the "Unusual Summer Camps" article. How did the strategy help you read and understand the selection? Tell how the strategy might help you when you read or view other articles.

Read Like a Writer

You have been reading articles that give real information about interesting people and their activities.

TALK ABOUT IT!

- What do you notice about the way the news articles are written?

- Make a chart to show what you know about news articles. Add to the chart as you read and view more articles, and create your own.

HINT!

Think about the audience. What **ideas** and **details** make the article interesting for them?

Articles
- headline is short and hooks readers' interest
- photos show action
- start with most important information
- use people's exact words
- include specific details
- leave readers with something to think about

Ultimate Fun

by Chelsea Donaldson

Is a Frisbee a toy or sports equipment?

Looking for a different kind of activity? What about a game that combines the fancy jumps and quick turnarounds of basketball, the long bomb passing of football, and the non-stop running of soccer?

If that appeals to you, you might want to try Ultimate Frisbee. What? You've never heard of it? Well, pay attention—you'll likely be hearing a lot more about this fast-growing sport in the years to come.

Ultimate Frisbee (or just Ultimate) is played on a field with two end zones, like football. Two teams of seven people try to score by passing the disc down the field to the other team's end zone. The player who has the disc cannot run. He or she must throw it to a teammate. If the teammate misses the pass or the other team gets it, play goes back the other way.

Sound like fun? It is. Today, more than 100 000 players in over 40 countries compete in organized clubs. Many others play in local leagues, or with friends. That's not bad for a sport that is only about 40 years old.

The History of the Frisbee

Of course, there would be no Ultimate without the Frisbee. And there would be no Frisbee without…pie? The first Frisbee was a tin pie plate from the Frisbie Pie Company in the United States. College students used to buy the pies and then toss the plates around—after they had eaten the contents, of course! In 1951, the Wham-O Toy Company started marketing plastic discs. At first, they were called "Pluto Platters." The name was changed to Frisbee in 1958. By 1967, Frisbees were popular all over North America. That's when a group of students at a high school in New Jersey decided to create a new game using the flying discs. Over the course of the next year, Ultimate was born. When the students graduated and went to college, they introduced the game to other students. Soon, the game spread to other colleges in other countries.

Canadians Rule!

Ultimate may have started out as an American sport, but Canadian teams have made up for lost time.

At the 2004 World Ultimate Championships, Canadian teams ranked first or second in every category. The Women's team not only won the top prize (for the second time), they did not lose a single game! The Men's team and the Junior Women also won Gold.

Canadian teams compete at the 2004 World Ultimate Championships, which were held in Finland.

Lara proudly wears the gold medals she's won at World Ultimate Championships.

Lara Mussell Savage

The captain of the undefeated Women's team in 2004 was Lara Mussell Savage. Lara is a member of the Skwah First Nation. She began playing Ultimate in high school. In 1998 she joined Prime, the Vancouver Women's team. Over the next eight years, Lara went on to become a two-time world champion and three-time Canadian champion. She also coached Ultimate Frisbee teams at university.

In 2005, Lara won the Tom Longboat Award. This award is given every year to the most outstanding male and female Aboriginal athletes in Canada.

The Canadian Women's and Men's teams celebrate after receiving their gold medals at the 2004 World Ultimate Championships.

Lara closely guards another player during the 2004 World Ultimate Championships.

The Spirit Factor

One thing that makes Ultimate unique is a factor known as Spirit of the Game (SOTG). SOTG means putting fair play ahead of everything—even winning. This attitude is important because there are no referees in Ultimate. Teams have to settle any arguments on their own. Players can even call a foul on themselves!

Good sportsmanship is so important that, in many tournaments, the "Spirit Award" is one of the highest honours a team can earn. The most important thing in Ultimate is that everyone has a good time.

So, what do you think? Are you ready for some fun? If so, pull on your sneakers, grab a few friends, and start throwing a disc around! It seems like just about *everyone* is doing it!

DIG DEEPER

1. With a partner or group, design a new Frisbee sport. Write the rules. Include a sketch or diagram. Present your sport to a group.

2. Make a chart or diagram comparing Ultimate Frisbee to another team sport.

Ultimate Frisbee	Soccer

Creating Visions

by Surya Bhattacharya

READ LIKE A WRITER

How does the author use Molly's own words to make the article more interesting?

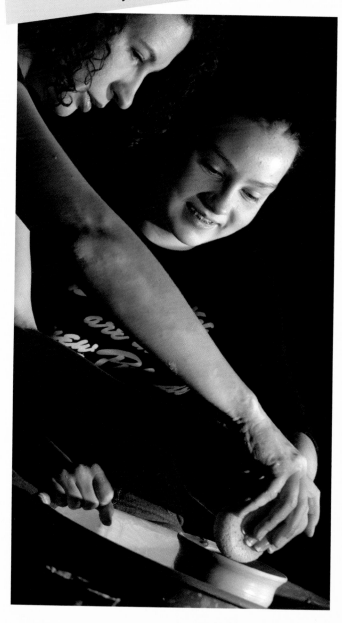

How can your hands help you "see"?

Eleven-year-old Molly Burke loves making cups and bowls, but she doesn't want to get her painted nails dirty in pottery class. When some polish flakes off, she notices it right away and peels off the rest. She holds it up for instructor Alexandra Travnickova and her mother to see. Then she brings it up close to her eyes to see what it looks like.

At the age of five, Molly started to lose her vision. Her eyes don't let in enough light for her to see well. Her condition is called "tunnel vision." Molly's mother explains it as something that "eats away" at part of her eye.

Molly Burke works on a sculpture with Alexandra Travnickova.

23

"That's a nice way to put it," says Molly with a grin. She explains that, along with tunnel vision, she also struggles to see through coloured spots that are always in front of her eyes.

But none of this stops her from going to pottery classes at Blind Kids Art. This is an organization started by Alexandra, and classes are held once a week. Alexandra helps children one at a time so she can watch them carefully. Each class is two hours long. Right now, Blind Kids Art has seven students aged 4 to 13.

Instruction takes longer because Alexandra has to explain everything she sees to the students. "The good thing is that they have superb memory," she says.

Some students were born blind, some have limited vision, and some, like Molly, have tunnel vision. "No one has complained that they can't see what they're doing," the teacher says.

To make a pot, Alexandra has Molly run her fingers over a sample pot a number of times. She slows down to explain details, such as the pot's curves, or how deep it is.

Molly announces she would like to be an actress when she grows up. "I think about it a lot," she says. "It's going to be harder for me, and things are going to get in the way," she says of her possible careers. These include acting and pottery.

In the meantime she enjoys a number of other activities.

Alexandra guides a student in her pottery class.

"It keeps me busy," says Molly of her many hobbies, which include acting and singing, playing the drums, horseback riding, and downhill skiing. "If I am not busy, I am bored." She'd like to snowboard, too, but unlike skiing, "they don't have guides on snowboards."

"Oh, and pottery," Molly adds. "I like that, too."

Alexandra helps a student use a potter's wheel.

Some of the pottery made by Alexandra's students.

DIG DEEPER

1. Use the 5W's to summarize this article: Who? What? When? Where? Why?

2. Write a new headline for this article.

Who?	
What?	
When?	
Where?	
Why?	

Reporters at Work!

You are going to interview someone in your class about one of their hobbies or interests. Then, you will write a one-page article for a class news collection.

Plan Your Interview

- Work with a partner.
- Make a list of questions you can ask to find out about special hobbies or activities.
- Share your questions with the class.
- Choose five questions you will ask.
- Leave space after each question to record answers.

TIPS FOR QUESTIONS

- Look back at the articles in this unit. What questions do you think the reporters asked?
- Think of the 5W's: Who? What? When? Where? Why?

Interview Your Partner

- Start with an easy question.
- Don't rush—give lots of time for the answers.
- Use jot notes to get the main points.
- Record the exact words if you are going to use a quote.
- Support and encourage your partner.

Write Your Article

- Think about your audience.
- Start with a catchy "lead" sentence.
- Use short paragraphs.
- Use some exact words from the person you interviewed.
- Work with an editing partner to make sure your writing is clear.

Publish Your Article

- Create a headline.
- Include an interesting photograph.
- Leave margins, and space your work so it's easy to read.
- Put your article with the class collection for students and visitors to share.

CHECK CONVENTIONS

- Have you used correct punctuation to show the exact words of a speaker?
- Are all your sentences complete?

MEOW! Josh's Kitten Wins Prize!

by Keisha Hardin
Staff Reporter

Josh Kim's kitten, Hairball, won the "Cutest Kitty" prize at the Lakeview Mall last weekend. The contest was sponsored by the Pets-Are-Us store in the mall. The prize was made up of $50.00 in cat food and a trophy with a silver cat on the top.

Josh says he didn't think his kitten had a chance of winning. "When I got there with Hairball, there must have been at least 50 other people there with their pets. I thought there was no way we would win!" said Josh. Josh entered anyway, and was excited when he and his kitten made it to the finals. "They chose 5 kittens to be in the finals," Josh explained. "That was when I got thinking we might have a chance."

The judges said they chose Hairball as the winner because of her bright green eyes and the interesting jigsaw pattern on her back. She was also behaved very well and didn't

Hairball (left) and Jujube rest together on Josh's couch.

meow and try to get away, like some of the other cats.

Josh and his family adopted Hairball and Hairball's sister, Jujube, from the Humane Society last month. The family also has a dog, Bandit.

The win has made Josh even more interested in becoming a vet. "I have always loved animals, says Josh. "When I saw all those animals together, it made me want to become a vet even more so I can help all animals."

Weird Zone

Strange and True Cool Collections

**by Maria Birmingham
and Guinness World Records™**

READ LIKE A WRITER
How does the author use details to show how unusual the collections are?

What weird hobbies do some people have?

It's a Wrap

You might say Gary Duschl is all wrapped up in his hobby. He's been collecting gum wrappers since 1965. Back then, his classmates were making gum wrapper chains, and 14-year-old Gary decided to make the longest one in his class. Today, Gary has collected more than one million wrappers, and his gum wrapper chain is the longest in the world. It's the length of 143 football fields! Donations from family, friends, and people who visit his Web site help Gary add 72 wrappers a day to his collection. Stick with it, Gary!

A Sign of the Times

Most people plant flowers in their gardens, but John Rietveld has traffic lights and road signs in his. Over the past 21 years, John has bought more than 70 traffic signals—the ones in his garden actually light up—as well as 600 road signs!

Gnome Sweet Gnome

Painter Ann Atkin is so crazy about garden gnomes that she's collected a record-breaking 2000 gnome figures over the past 25 years. And what's more, she's opened a Gnome Reserve where she displays her collection among gardens and ponds. Visitors can wear gnome hats and wander around the reserve looking at scenes like the "Gnome Beach," which features gnomes sunbathing on the sand and fishing off a pier. Go figure!

29

Daffy for Ducks!

Charlotte Lee owns 1439 different rubber ducks, which she has collected since 1996. Charlotte began her collection when she bought a pack of three rubber ducks for her bathroom. The following week she bought another three to keep them company. Friends who saw these were so amused that they began to give her ducks as gifts.

"I don't have a favourite duck," says Charlotte when asked. "I love them all!"

Take a Seat

Who needs paint and a canvas to create masterpieces? For more than 30 years, 82-year-old Barney Smith has transformed toilet seats into works of art. This retired plumber has created more than 640 pieces of toilet seat art, all of which hang in his garage. There's a toilet seat plastered with pictures of dogs, others with souvenirs from vacations, and still another covered in jigsaw puzzle pieces. Each creation is so special to him that he hasn't parted with even one over the years. Potty on!

It's a Small World

David Weingarten doesn't have to travel far to visit the world's most famous buildings. He can head to the shed behind his home. That's where he keeps his collection of 3000 miniature toy buildings. Over the past 20 years, David has collected mini replicas of everything from the Empire State Building to Big Ben to the pyramids. David's collection features buildings from nearly 1200 places around the globe. Some of the miniatures are even useful, like the Eiffel Tower that's also a pencil sharpener and the bank building that doubles as a piggy bank!

DIG DEEPER

1. Choose one of the weird collections. With a partner, role-play an interview with the collector.
2. Imagine another type of weird collection. Write and illustrate a description. Use the article as a model.

Numbers Talk

From dinosaur bones to moon rocks, museums house some of the biggest collections in the world.

Smithsonian Institution
Washington, DC, U.S.

More than
140 million
objects in 14 museums

Royal Ontario Museum
Toronto, ON, Canada

More than
5 million objects

The State Hermitage Museum
St. Petersburg, Russia

More than
3 million objects

MEDIA WATCH

Look for newspaper or television news stories about weird collections or other unusual activities. Why does the media include stories like these?

What Do Canadian Kids Like to Do?

by the Canadian Teachers' Federation
Illustrated by Dave Whamond

READ LIKE A WRITER

How do the graphs make the information quick and easy to understand?

What hobbies and activities do Canadian kids enjoy?

Researchers asked Grade 4 students from across Canada this question:

It's the weekend and you have a few hours to do whatever you want. What would you do?

The next two graphs show the survey results for 100 girls and 100 boys.

What would *your* answer be?

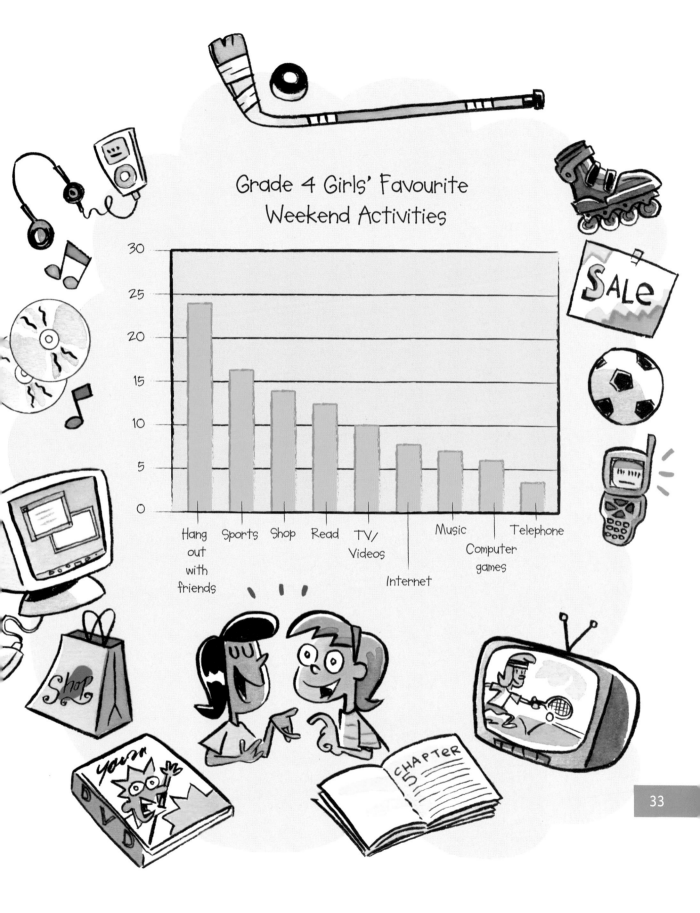

Grade 4 Girls' Favourite Weekend Activities

Grade 4 Boys' Favourite Weekend Activities

Students were also asked how often they did hobbies, took music or other lessons, or went to organized groups like Scouts or Guides. Students could answer that they did these things:

- Almost never
- A few times a month
- A few times a week
- Almost every day

Here are the results for 100 Grade 4 girls and 100 Grade 4 boys.

How Often Girls Do Hobbies, Take Lessons, or Go to Groups like Scouts or Guides

How Often Boys Do Hobbies, Take Lessons, or Go to Groups like Scouts or Guides

36

DIG DEEPER

1. With a partner, make up your own question about hobbies or other activities, then survey your class. Present your results in a graph like the ones in this article.

2. Create a four-panel cartoon showing one of your favourite activities. Include speech and thought balloons.

WOW – WHAT A RECORD!

by Guinness World Records™
Illustrated by Dave Whamond

What unusual records have Canadians set?

Making something larger, longer, or taller than anyone else takes imagination. It also takes a lot of planning. Here are some records that Canadians have set.

READ LIKE A WRITER
How does the author use specific details to explain the records?

Largest Group Hug

A total of 5117 students, staff, and friends met at St. Matthew's Secondary School in Orleans, Ontario, on April 23, 2004. They hugged each other for 10 seconds to raise money for a local cancer charity.

Longest Hot Wheels Track

The longest Hot Wheels track measured 502.92 m. It was made up of 2100 pieces of track, held together by 2150 connectors. The attempt was organized by Mattel Canada, Inc., for Big Brothers Big Sisters of Canada. The track was completed on July 7, 2002, in Toronto, Ontario.

Youngest Radio Host

On January 16, 1999, Cody Morton hosted a show on CHOO FM in Tofino, British Columbia. He was 10 years, 218 days old at the time.

Largest Finger Painting

A finger painting measuring 473.8 m^2 was completed on July 22, 2003. Its creation was led by artists Jignesh Patel and Munir Rehman on behalf of the people of Surrey Central, British Columbia.

DIG DEEPER

1. With a group, brainstorm a list of record-setting activities that the students in your class could try. Make sure the activities are safe and suitable for everyone.

2. If you could set any record in the world, what one would you choose? Write a paragraph telling about your choice.

Tallest Ridable Bicycle

Terry Goertzen rode the world's tallest bicycle on June 26, 2004, in Winnipeg, Manitoba. His bicycle was 5.5 m tall. Terry rode it for a distance of over 300 m.

Skateboard

by John Grandits

I'm on my totally cool new board and I'm *bombing the hill.* I do a little cut jump up a **curb** into the

I do a little cut jump up a

lift onto the bench,

Out of the lot, *curb,* *across the street,* *curb,* into the park. I do a sweet little

Busted. Walking home. I'm a sad old dog who's been swatted with a rolled-up newspaper.

1. Read the poem with a partner. One of you read the lines in black type, and the other the lines in red.

2. Write and illustrate a poem about one of your favourite hobbies or activities.

milk crate when all of a sudden I hear HEY, KID!
No skateboards
in the
parking lot.
Get outta here!

7-Eleven parking lot and try a tight little figure eight just to see how she corner's, and I'm about to try a tricky little ollie over a

up the hill, around the flagpole,
p
m-
u-
u-
u-
land clean, p-

d-
o-
o-
o-
w-
n the ramp, and HEY, YOU!
Can't you read the sign?
No skateboarding!

I give up. I'm just gonna

veg in front of the TV
and not think about it.

I mean, why bother, and then HEY,
What are you doing inside?
You begged for that
skateboard, Robert.
Now go out and use it!

41

Live from L E G

Why do people like to build models?

42

Tourists admire a town made of LEGO blocks at LEGOLAND in Denmark.

DIG DEEPER

1. With a group, make a chart showing hobbies that involve building or making something. Make a sketch for each hobby.

Hobby	Sketch

2. Choose a hobby from your chart that you enjoy or would like to try. Create a story for a newspaper or TV program about your choice.

Abracadabra, a Chain of Clips!

by Peter Eldin

READ LIKE A WRITER

How does the writer help readers follow the steps of the magic trick?

Are there secrets behind the hobby of doing magic tricks?

In this stunning trick, show five ordinary paper clips to the audience, then tip them into an empty hat. When you take them out, your audience will be amazed to see that the clips have linked themselves together by magic!

Get Ready

You will need:

10 paper clips

a book (hardcover)

a hat

1. Link five clips together and push them into the spine of the book. If you use coloured paper clips, make sure that the ones in the chain are the same colour as the single ones.

2. Put the book on your table, open at the middle pages.

3. Put the five loose clips into the hat.

Perform the Trick

1. Tip the loose clips from the hat into your hand. (This proves that the hat is otherwise empty without you having to draw any special attention to the fact.)

2. Count the clips one at a time onto the book to show that they are all separate.

3 Pick up the book and, keeping it low down, tip the clips back into the hat. The linked clips will also fall into the hat from their secret hiding place in the book spine.

4 Wave your hands over the hat in a mysterious manner and then pick up the first clip in the chain.

5 Pull out the chain of clips, leaving the loose clips hidden in the hat, as your audience applauds.

TOP TIP

You can use the same idea to make money multiply. Secretly hide two coins in the book spine. Borrow two coins from people in the audience, put them on the book, and tip them into the hat. At the same time, the coins you put in the spine of the book will fall out. Take out the four coins, and return the borrowed coins to their owners. Put the two extra ones into your pocket and say that this is the way magicians make money!

DIG DEEPER

1. Work with a partner to practise and perform the magic trick.

2. This selection is a procedure. It tells readers *how* to do something. Make a chart comparing the ways that procedures and news articles are written.

Procedures	News articles

The Chinese Violin

MADELEINE THIEN • ILLUSTRATED BY JOE CHANG

How can the things you love to do connect you to other people?

READ LIKE A WRITER

How does the illustrator help readers understand and visualize the story?

Lin Lin used to play on a grassy hill in her small village in China. On Sunday afternoons, people came from far and wide with their violins and flutes and mandolins. Lin Lin and her father would sit among the butterflies and birds and flowers and listen to the music. Lin Lin loved her small village.

Sometimes, Lin Lin and her father floated the day away on the river. He would play the violin, and Lin Lin would try to play it too.

Afterward, she would close her eyes and listen to the sounds—the frogs singing, the children laughing, the drifting cry of the violin.

Lin Lin's father loved their small village too, but he said it was time to leave China. One night, he filled out papers so they could move to Canada. When the papers were approved, he picked Lin Lin up in his arms and lifted her high in the air. Lin Lin pretended to be excited, but in her heart she was frightened.

Before they left, Lin Lin walked through her village one last time. She stood very still and listened to the birds and the flutes, and the wind moving on the grassy hill. The song from a violin drifted toward her. Lin Lin wanted to keep the village in her memory forever.

When they arrived in Vancouver, Lin Lin was surprised by the sounds. Hollering seagulls dipped across the sky. The noises of the cars and people and a new language swept over Lin Lin like an ocean.

At school, the children called to each other in English and
played games Lin Lin had never seen before. She stood by
herself, listening to their laughter float across the playground.
She looked up at the big blue sky, but even the sky felt like a
stranger.

Lin Lin's father decided they needed something to lift their spirits. "Lin Lin," he said. "Let's go to the park today. Everyone says the park will make us feel at home again." She followed her father through the city, through the trees, all the way to the ocean. Lin Lin's father unwrapped his violin and leaned it against his knee. When he played the first notes, Lin Lin felt her heart singing.

Lin Lin fell asleep and dreamed a wonderful dream. She was soaring high in the clouds. When she looked down, she could see her small village and this new city and the deep blue ocean between them. When Lin Lin awoke, her father was playing the violin. The music filled the air around her. Lin Lin leaned against her father and hoped that one day she would be able to play the violin as beautifully as he did. For the next few weeks, Lin Lin remembered that feeling of soaring among the clouds. School was hard, but the memory comforted her.

One afternoon, she and her father walked downtown. On a busy corner, he unwrapped his violin and leaned it against his knee. He played a beautiful song.

People came and stood in a circle around him. They closed their eyes and listened to the music. When her father finished, they cheered and clapped. They left coins in the cardboard box that Lin Lin had set on the ground.

That evening, Lin Lin and her father set out for home through the meandering streets. She held her father's hand and listened to the coins jingling in the box and the reassuring sound around her of her father's shoes on the pavement.

Suddenly, two men came out of the shadows and grabbed Lin Lin's father. She screamed and yelled at them to stop. The men took her father's wallet, and the cardboard box fell to the ground, spilling coins everywhere. The men ran away.

On the sidewalk, Lin Lin's father put his face in his hands and wept. The violin was cracked and broken. Lin Lin wrapped her arms around her father's neck and held him tight.

Over the next few weeks, Lin Lin tried to concentrate on her schoolwork, but her mind was full. She remembered her small village and the music of the violin drifting across the grassy hill. She tried to read her English books, but the words swam in front of her eyes.

All day long, Lin Lin's father worked at his new job. He washed dishes in a busy restaurant. At night he helped Lin Lin with her schoolwork. "Don't worry," he told her. "Very soon this place will feel like home."

When Lin Lin saw how hard her father was trying, she didn't want to disappoint him. At school, the teacher helped Lin Lin with her English words. Lin Lin imagined that soon all the words would roll off her tongue and she would be able to laugh and sing alongside the other children.

One day, Lin Lin's father surprised her with a present. "Lin Lin," he said. "I know you have been studying very hard. I have found something special for you." In his hands was a new violin.

Lin Lin's heart leapt. The violin reminded Lin Lin of her dream. She remembered flying in the clouds, through the big sky. She clutched the violin and jumped into her father's arms.

By autumn, Lin Lin could play an entire song. She practised outside, beneath the big trees and their tumbling leaves. One by one, her friends came to listen. It didn't matter that she was shy when she spoke. They loved the sound of her music.

Every time Lin Lin missed her small village, she played the violin. The music drifted in the air along with the calling of the birds and the sound of the wind in the trees.

One day, in the school auditorium, Lin Lin played the violin for an audience. When she heard the notes, she felt herself soaring with the music, lifted up by all the familiar faces.

In the front row, her father beamed at her. Lin Lin saw his happy face and heard the sound of her own heart singing.

DIG DEEPER

1. Make a web showing how the Chinese violin connected Lin Lin to her memories and to other people.

2. Write a journal entry telling about some music that is important to you, and why.

Birth of a Birder

by Robert Bateman

READ LIKE A WRITER

What details does Robert Bateman include to show how important birds are to him?

How did a famous painter become "hooked" on bird watching?

It started with a Black-capped Chickadee. I was eight years old; the place was a country lane north of Toronto, where I grew up. On that cold November day, something caught my eye. It was a lively little ball of fluff, hopping from twig to twig in a leafless hedge. I forgot about the cold as I watched the agile little bird with the black cap and white cheeks.

I don't know why, but from that moment I was hooked. Soon I was spending hours in the ravine behind my house. I inched through bushes with my ears and eyes wide open. It was an adventure.

I hope seeing some of my favourite birds will launch you on your own adventure. Of all wild creatures, birds are the most colourful and the easiest to see. You don't need to travel to distant jungles or faraway islands. They live in our backyards. If you just spend time watching and listening, you will discover them. Birds are our neighbours. We should get to know them.

56

Black-capped Chickadee

Length: 13 cm

Wingspan: 20 cm

Weight: 12 g

Voice: Common and familiar call is *chickadee-dee-dee-dee*

Food: Spiders, insects, seeds (especially sunflower seeds), and berries

Range: Northern U.S. and most of Canada

Habitat: Forests, thickets, groves, and residential areas

Red-winged Blackbird

Length: 22 cm

Wingspan: 33 cm

Weight: 51 g

Voice: Gurgling trill kon-ka-reee

Food: Insects while breeding; fruit and grains the rest of the year

Range: North America

Habitat: Marshes and brushy swamps; wet areas near farmland

Red-tailed Hawk

Length: 48 cm

Wingspan: 125 cm

Weight: 1.1 kg

Voice: A hoarsely screamed *tsseee-arr*

Food: Small mammals such as rabbits, mice, and rats

Range: Most of the U.S. and Canada up to the Arctic

Habitat: Mixed country of pastures or fields with nearby trees; often perched along roads

DIG DEEPER

1. Imagine that you are a bird who enjoys watching people. From the bird's point of view, write about an experience as a "people watcher."

2. Make field notes about a type of bird in your community. Include a sketch and description, and tell when and where you observed it.

Connect and Share

People make scrapbooks about things that are important to them. Scrapbooks can include drawings, photographs, artifacts, and captions.

Gather materials!

- Choose a special interest or hobby you enjoy, or one you would like to try.
- With your family, find or draw pictures about your choice.
- Find other objects you can add to the page.
- Bring your pictures and objects to school.

TIPS
- Think about your main message.
- Use interesting lettering.
- Try adding a border.

Make a scrapbook page!

- Make captions on separate pieces of paper.
- Try different ways of arranging your pictures before you glue them.
- Show your own special personality!
- Share your scrapbook page with your family.

Spotlight on Learning

Collect

- Gather your interview notes, notebooks, articles, pictures, and other work you did in this unit. Include your planning notes and reflections for oral activities.

Talk and reflect

Work with a partner.

- Together, read the Learning Goals on page 2.
- Talk about how well you met these goals.
- Look through your work for evidence.

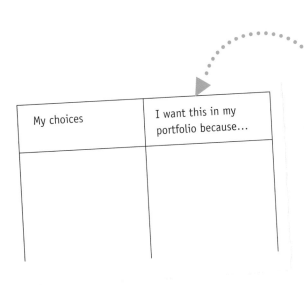

My choices	I want this in my portfolio because...

Select

- Choose two pieces of work that show how you achieved the Learning Goals. (The same piece of work can show more than one goal.)

Tell about your choices

- Tell what each piece shows about your learning.

Reflect

- What have you learned about reading, listening to, and viewing news articles?
- What have you learned about creating them?

61

Make Me Laugh!

LEARNING GOALS

In this unit you will:

- Read, view, and listen to humorous stories.

- Make predictions, inferences, and connections about what you read and view.

- Create and share jokes, plays, and stories.

- Reflect on the skills and strategies you are learning.

- Contribute to group discussions and activities.

jokester
riddles
comedians
humour
comical
ROFL (rolling on the
floor laughing)

63

Awful Ogre Takes His Supper

by Jack Prelutsky
Illustrated by Paul O. Zelinsky

What funny
events might
happen at Awful
Ogre's supper?

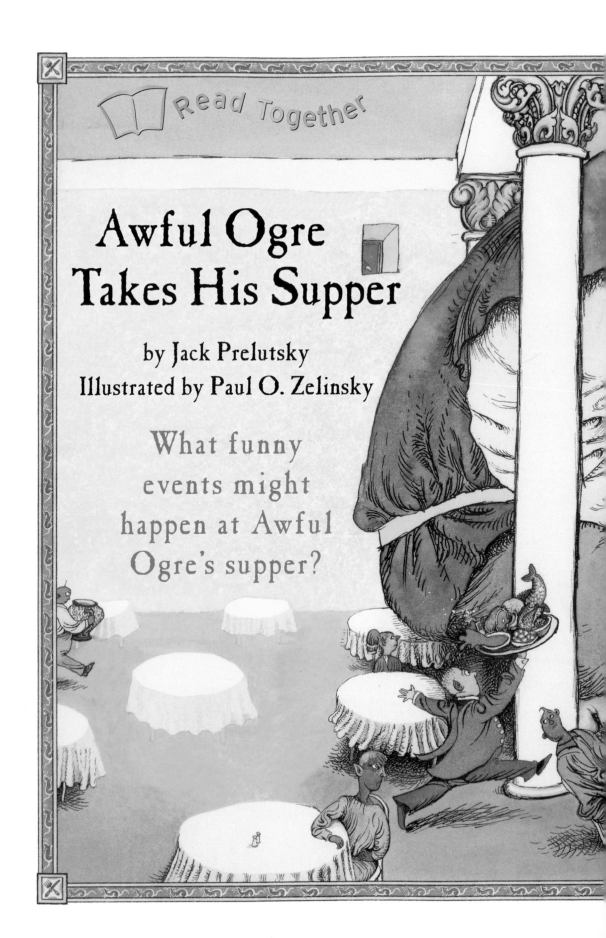

When I don't feel like cooking,
And supper time is near,
I step out to a restaurant
Just forty miles from here.
No matter if they're crowded,
They always seat me first,
Then bring me pails of water
To alleviate my thirst.

I never need a menu,

They empty every pot

And rush me triple portions

Of everything they've got.

Should that prove insufficient,

I simply start to roar…

They whip up extra helpings

And serve me more and more.

I wolf down all they proffer

Till not a scrap remains.

The other patrons notice,

But none of them complains.

They gaze in fascination

As I savour every bite,

Feeling privileged to witness

My titanic appetite.

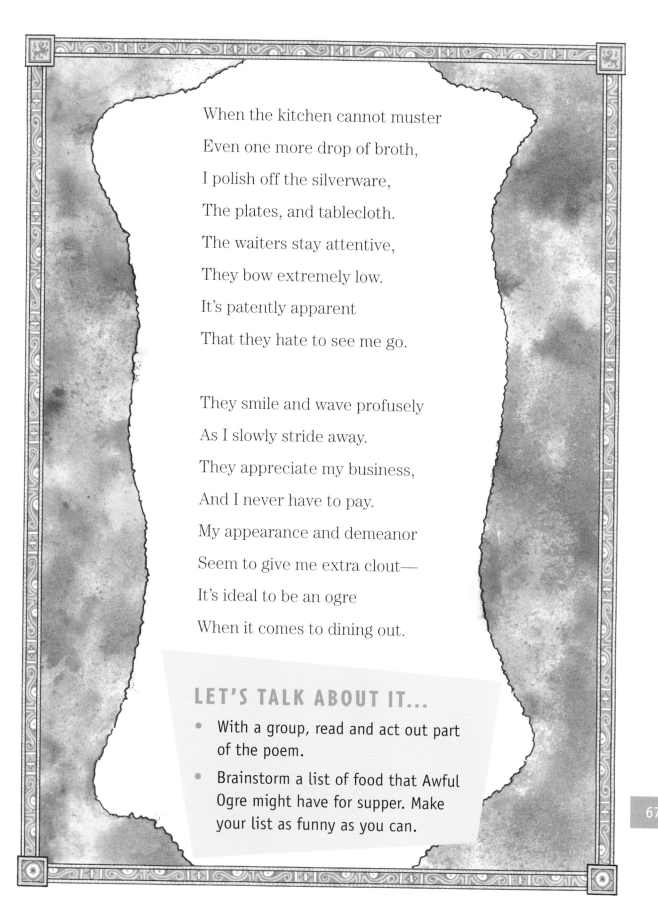

When the kitchen cannot muster

Even one more drop of broth,

I polish off the silverware,

The plates, and tablecloth.

The waiters stay attentive,

They bow extremely low.

It's patently apparent

That they hate to see me go.

They smile and wave profusely

As I slowly stride away.

They appreciate my business,

And I never have to pay.

My appearance and demeanor

Seem to give me extra clout—

It's ideal to be an ogre

When it comes to dining out.

LET'S TALK ABOUT IT...

- With a group, read and act out part of the poem.

- Brainstorm a list of food that Awful Ogre might have for supper. Make your list as funny as you can.

Read Fictional Stories

Fictional stories are stories that didn't really happen. They can be told in words, actions, and pictures.

Think about a fictional story or cartoon that made you laugh.

- What was the story about?

TALK ABOUT IT!

- Share your story with a partner.
- Talk about what made it funny.
- Where can you find other funny stories?

  Here are some clues.

Make a chart together.

| Funny Stories | |
Where you find them	Examples

Think Like a Reader

I've never heard of patrons before. But from what comes before and after, I think it means customers in the restaurant.

Read with a purpose

- Why do you read funny stories?

Crack the code

Readers often figure out new words by using context clues. They look at what comes before and after the word they don't know. Then they think about what makes sense.

Make meaning

Practise using these strategies when you read stories:

PREDICT   Look at the title and pictures. Think about what you know about stories.

INFER   Read between the lines to figure out what people are thinking or feeling.

CONNECT   Think about how the story connects to other stories you have read or seen.

Analyze what you read

- What makes a story funny?
- Why are some stories funny to some people and not funny to other people?

To the Pole!

PREDICT

What "Pole" do you think people are going to?

INFER

How does Soon Jin feel when she hears the howling?

Mandy, Soon Jin, Josh, and Amir were busy building a snow fort.

"Let's pretend we're searching for the South Pole," said Mandy.

"I'll go ahead to explore!" cried Soon Jin. She set off down Fenton Street in the heavily falling snow.

"*Woow-woow!*"

"Listen! Wolves are howling!" she heard Mandy say from behind her.

As she moved down the street, Soon Jin heard more howling. "*Wooooow-wooooow!*" Those wolves sounded close. They sounded hungry. They sounded dangerous!

"Soon Jin? Is that you?" She lifted her snow-covered eyelashes to see her neighbour, Mrs. Graves.

"Are you all right, dear?" asked Mrs. Graves.

"I'm all right," said Soon Jin bravely. "I'm an explorer searching for the Pole."

"Searching for the pole?" asked Mrs. Graves. "Well, I'm searching for something too. But you're luckier than I am, because the pole's right here." She placed Soon Jin's hands on a nearby telephone pole and went on her way.

"I guess I've found the Pole," Soon Jin muttered. "I must tell the rest of the Fenton Street Four the good news!"

She turned and began her journey back, then heard the howl of the wolves again. "*Wooow-wooow!*"

Suddenly something dark and furry slammed against her, thumping her into a snow bank.

"Awk!" she yelled hoarsely.

Right above her nose was a huge furry face, a large red mouth, and pointed white teeth.

She tried to cover her head, but a huge pink tongue was slobbering all over her face.

Soon Jin looked up and saw her friends with their arms around the animal. Were they hugging and petting a wolf? Were they crazy?

Soon Jin looked again. It was no wolf. It was her neighbour's dog!

"Muffy!" cried Soon Jin. Muffy's tail wagged furiously. "Now I know what Mrs. Graves was searching for!"

CONNECT

How does this story remind you of other stories you know?

Mountain Tamers

Amir peered out the window down Fenton Street. Then he turned and asked his mom for the fifth time, "When do you think Grandma will be here?"

Amir would soon be ten. He had asked for just one gift, a Mountain Tamer sled. He had seen it in a store flyer, and his grandma had said she would get it for him. These sleds were purple with red flames along the sides. The kids all knew they were the fastest sleds around.

At last Amir spied his grandma. He quickly put on his jacket and boots and raced out to her car. As he got close, he saw her pulling from the trunk…a white-and-pink sled called the Snow Flake! Amir stared in horror.

His grandma gave him a big hug. "Happy birthday, Amir!" she said. "Now, I know this is not exactly the sled you wanted. It was sold out. But this is almost the same."

Amir said quietly, "Thank you, Grandma." He hung his head. How could he be seen on a Snow Flake? He had told his friends he was getting a Mountain Tamer.

"But that's not all I got at the store," his grandma went on. "I also got *this*!" She held up rolls of bright red and orange tape. "I thought we could dress up your sled a bit. You know, make it your own."

Amir helped carry the sled into the garage. He and his grandma got to work.

Some time later, he heard the rest of the Fenton Street Four coming to call for him.

"I'm in here!" he called out to them.

Mandy, Soon Jin, and Josh opened the garage door and gasped. There sat the coolest sled any of them had ever seen. There were zigzags of red lightning along both sides. Bright orange flames covered the front. There were even wings made of red tape sticking out the back.

"Wow!" gasped Josh. "That's the most awesome sled I've ever seen. Can we take turns on it?"

Amir hugged his grandma and said, "Sure! *This* will be how the Fenton Street Four tames a mountain!"

INFER

How does Amir feel when his grandma gives him the sled?

CONNECT

How does this story remind you of other stories you know?

The Science of Snow Fun

Mandy wiped the steam from the window and looked out. She could see the rest of the Fenton Street Four out in the park, running and laughing. It was snowing again!

"I'm off to play, Dad!" she called. She put on her warmest clothes and raced down the hall and out the door of her apartment building.

"Hey, Mandy!" Josh yelled when he saw her. "It's snowing marshmallows!"

"It's snowing *what*?"

"Marshmallows! They're falling from the sky!" yelled Josh, stretching his arms high in the air.

"Those aren't marshmallows," said Mandy. "Marshmallows are round. Snowflakes have six sides."

"But snowflakes are white like marshmallows."

"No," said Mandy slowly, "they're really clear. It's just that a bunch of them *look* white."

"Well, they're soft like marshmallows," said Amir, falling backwards with a *whump*. "And they look white, and they look round. So they *could* be marshmallows!" Then he laughed as he watched Soon Jin make a skunk stripe down Josh's back with a handful of snow.

"Just because something *looks* like something doesn't mean that's what it is," Mandy answered. "Snow comes from water vapour that freezes into crystals." She peered down at her sleeve. "Look! It's a bunch of crystals!"

74

She looked at her friends, eager to explain more. She wanted to tell them how these large snowflakes were likely formed in low clouds, and how snowflakes formed in higher, colder clouds were different. But now her friends were all on the ground, ready to roll like logs down the park's small hill.

"Come on, Mandy," Josh laughed. "This will be fun!"

"Make room for me!" another boy yelled as he barrelled his way to the top of the slope, ready to roll.

Mandy thought for a moment. Then she shouted, "Hey! Wait for me!"

She raced to join her friends. The science of snow might be fun to her. But, right now, *playing* in snow looked even *more* fun!

With loud screams, the Fenton Street Four rolled down the hill together.

INFER

How do Mandy's friends feel about her explanation of snow?

CONNECT

How does this story remind you of other stories you know?

75

Reflect on Your Reading

You have . . .

- talked about your favourite funny stories.
- thought about what makes a story funny.
- practised using context clues to figure out new words.

jokester   riddles   comedians
humour   comical
ROFL

You have also . . .

- explored different reading strategies.

My favourite funny stories are cartoons with animal characters. I like the voices they give the characters. What are your favourites?

PREDICT
INFER
CONNECT

Write About Learning

Write about one of the strategies you used when you read the selection "The Fenton Street Four." How did the strategy help you read and understand the selection? Tell how the strategy might help you when you read other kinds of stories.

Read Like a Writer

When authors create fictional stories, they make up the events that happen. In a humorous story, they try to create funny events.

TALK ABOUT IT!

- What do you notice about the stories about the Fenton Street Four?
- Think of other stories you have read or written.
- Make a chart to show what you know about stories.

HINT!

Look at how authors choose their **words** and **phrases** to give a mood or feeling.

Stories
- start in an interesting way
- have descriptive language
- use details to make you feel like you are there
- tell events in order
- have the most exciting part near the end

The Biggest Scoop

Why **did** the chicken cross the road?

in the Coop

by Jeff Szpirglas
Illustrated by Dave Whamond

Cluck Kent slicked back his feathers and stared into the television camera. "Cluck Kent here, reporting live from the side of the road. A huge crowd has gathered behind me. And there's just one question on everyone's mind tonight: Why is the chicken going to cross the road?"

Standing nearby at the edge of the road was Rooster McDee, decked out in a snazzy-pants jogging suit and brand new runners. Rooster stretched his wings. He touched his toes.

He was almost ready, ready to finally cross the road.

No chicken in the entire history of the coop had ever dared to cross the road before. The road was always busy with cars and trucks zooming past. Crossing the road would be cracked, fried, and just plain scrambled.

If Cluck Kent could get an interview with Rooster, he would be the top TV reporter in the coop.

READ LIKE A WRITER

How do the author's words and phrases add humour to the story?

Featherweather's Revenge

Suddenly, a van from another news station cut off Cluck Kent before he reached Rooster. The van's door flew open and a news team spilled out. They were led by Cluck Kent's arch-enemy, ace reporter Barbara Featherweather.

Cluck Kent remembered the time he tried to interview Chicken Little about the sky falling. Barbara Featherweather had unplugged his microphone so nobody could hear it.

Back at the side of the road, Barbara Featherweather elbowed Cluck Kent out of the way. "Step aside. I'm about to do the greatest interview ever with Rooster McDee."

Cluck Kent pointed a proud wing at the big satellite dish perched on top of his news van.

"Yeah, but my interview with Rooster will be seen across the country in High-Definition Poultry Vision!" he huffed.

"Forget about your Poultry Vision. Our traffic chopper will film Rooster's crossing from high in the sky," clucked Barbara Featherweather, pointing to a helicopter hovering above.

Cluck Kent had to think quickly. "I've got something even better. I'm going to interview the people watching!" Cluck Kent yanked someone out of the crowd and pointed his microphone at her.

"Why is Rooster crossing the road? Is he trying to prove something? Is he crazy? Or is he just a rotten egg?" he asked the spectator.

"Two can play at that game!" flapped Barbara Featherweather, yanking someone else out of the crowd. "Who's a better reporter, Cluck Kent or me?"

The Big Showdown

By now, the crowd had turned away from Rooster. They were more interested in watching the two reporters fighting. Only the news helicopter pilot high in the sky saw Rooster look both ways, then take a step off the curb.

"The chicken is crossing the road!" the helicopter pilot shouted over a loudspeaker. "Repeat! The chicken is crossing the road!"

All eyes turned to the other side of the road.

The chicken had crossed. It was history in the making and everyone had missed it. The reporters could only watch breathlessly as Rooster looked both ways before crossing back again.

Gobble Squabble

Barbara Featherweather dropped her microphone. "But my cameras weren't rolling!"

"I let this story slip right through my feathers!" Cluck Kent moaned.

Barbara Featherweather shook her head. "Both of us did."

Just then, Cluck Kent got an idea so cracked, so fried, and so scrambled that it just might work. "We shouldn't be squabbling over our pecking order. Let's interview Rooster together."

The two reporters found Rooster and Cluck Kent fired off the first question: "Tell us, Rooster. Why did you cross the road?"

"To get to the other side?" Barbara Featherweather offered.

"To boldly go where no bird has gone before?" Cluck Kent tried.

"Sheesh!" Rooster responded. "You reporters make a story out of everything! I just wanted to break in my new running shoes. Now if you'll excuse me, I'm going for a little jog."

And, Rooster did just that, leaving the two reporters flabbergasted.

Barbara Featherweather shook her head. "You know what this story is?"

"A turkey," Cluck Kent shrugged. "But I'm sure our viewers will gobble it up."

MEDIA WATCH

Watch a television interview. Record who was interviewed and what the person did to be "newsworthy."

DIG DEEPER

1. Role-play a TV news broadcast of this event. Include an announcer as well as the reporters.

2. Create a funny animal character. Make a sketch or drawing. Include a caption that tells about your character.

Driving Mrs. Torpolli Crazy

by James Proimos

Mrs. Torpolli never really understood Johnny.

WHY DO YOU HAVE SOCKS ON YOUR EARS?

THEY LOOKED SILLY ON MY HANDS.

YOU CRAZY.

SHE'S SO HER.

READ LIKE A WRITER
Notice how the words and pictures work together to create humour in this story of Johnny Mutton.

But Johnny always loved her.

What kinds of things might upset Mrs. Torpolli?

One day Johnny decided he would make Mrs. Torpolli love him. He went to her store and told her so.

TODAY I WILL MAKE YOU LOVE ME.

SHEESH.

YOU WANT ME TO LOVE YOU? HMMM. PUTTING MR. STOCKMAN'S GROCERIES IN A BAG WOULDN'T HURT YOUR CHANCES.

I'M ON IT, SISTA!

Mutton bagged all that day.
He was awful at it.

LEARN FROM JOHNNY'S MISTAKES.

MR. STOCKMAN'S BAG

DON'T THROW EGGS IN ONE AT A TIME.

LORETTA SMATZ'S BAG

NEVER BREAK BREAD INTO TINY PIECES SO IT WON'T STICK OUT OF THE BAG.

RICO ZANZABAR'S BAG

NO NEED TO TEST THE MILK BEFORE PACKING IT.

VIVIAN BLANKHEAD'S BAG

IT'S SILLY TO POUR KETCHUP INTO THE BAG SO THE LADY WON'T HAVE TO CARRY A HEAVY BOTTLE.

GET OUT AND STAY OUT!

Mrs. Torpolli told Johnny never to enter her store again. She was very angry.

But all that night customers called
Mrs. Torpolli on the phone.

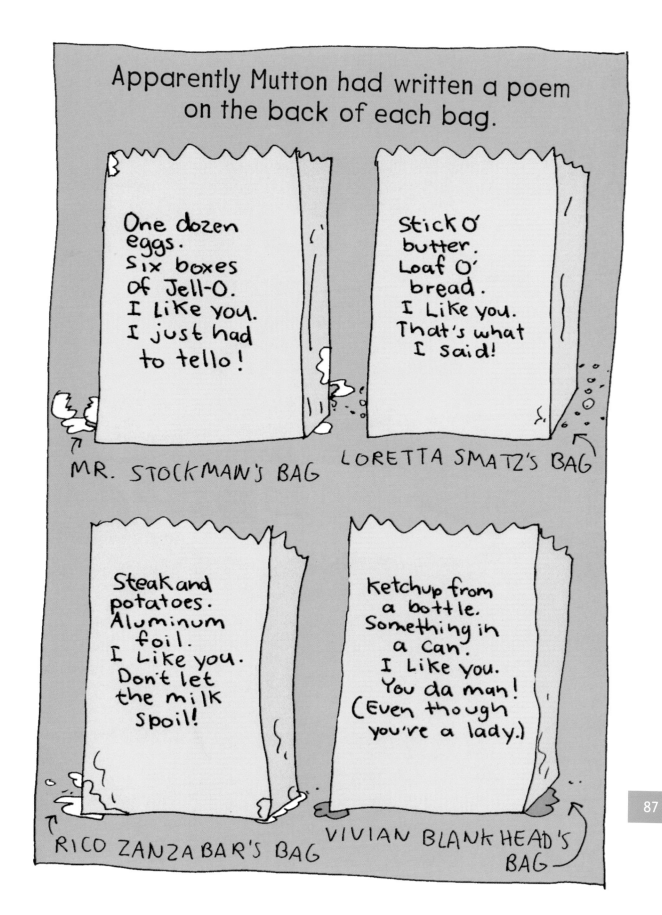

Apparently Mutton had written a poem on the back of each bag.

One dozen eggs.
Six boxes of Jell-O.
I like you.
I just had to tello!

MR. STOCKMAN'S BAG

Stick O' butter.
Loaf O' bread.
I like you.
That's what I said!

LORETTA SMATZ'S BAG

Steak and potatoes.
Aluminum foil.
I like you.
Don't let the milk spoil!

RICO ZANZABAR'S BAG

Ketchup from a bottle.
Something in a can.
I like you.
You da man!
(Even though you're a lady.)

VIVIAN BLANKHEAD'S BAG

The next day on her walk to work, Mrs. Torpolli figured out that Johnny had written all those poems for her.

DIG DEEPER . . . .

1. Write your own poem to one of Mrs. Torpolli's customers.

2. Draw one or two new cartoon panels about Johnny Mutton.

Jokin' Around

by Samara

How do you get to be a kid comedian?

My name is Samara. I love telling jokes and making people laugh. Come with me to see what it's like to be a kid comedian! Maybe you'll see me on TV someday, like other famous comedians!

The Funniest Kids Around

I perform with Kids 'n Comedy. We're a group of crazy kid jokesters. We take classes from real comedians on how to crack up a crowd. Only the funniest kids in the class get to perform at a stand-up comedy club in New York City. We get the audience laughing out loud when we perform our zany comedy routines.

READ LIKE A WRITER

How does Samara use different words for "funny" to keep the article interesting?

A Really Goofy Gal

So, how did I get to be a kid comedian? Well, my dad and I like to goof around. He'll crack a joke and I'll finish it. So, my dad thought I should try stand-up comedy. Most of the Kids 'n Comedy kids write their own jokes, but since I'm the youngest in the group, my dad and I work as a team. But, it won't be long before I'm writing all my own gut-busting stuff!

Me and the Kids 'n Comedy gang

How to be a stand-up comedian

Write down funny things you hear and see so you'll always have ideas for jokes.

Practise, practise, practise! Say the joke in the mirror until YOU find it funny.

If you mess up when you're telling a joke, just keep going!

If you look like you're having a good time, the audience will have fun too!

Let the Show Begin!

When I get on stage, it's really great to hear the audience laugh. I used to be pretty nervous when I first started performing. But I practise a lot, so now I'm always ready to get the audience howling. Hearing them laugh makes me want to do stand-up comedy forever. I think telling jokes is the best job you could have!

Jokin' around with my dad

What do you call a dog that likes to run all the time?

A jog dog!

DIG DEEPER

1. Work with a partner to choose and practise some jokes. Then put on a comedy show for a small group.

2. Imagine you are a kid comedian. Write about the best and the worst parts of being a kid comedian.

Best	Worst

Have You Heard This One?

What makes a joke funny?

What do you get when you cross a cow and a duck?

Milk and quackers.

Q Why do cows have bells?

A Because their horns don't work.

READ LIKE A WRITER

How do the knock-knock jokes use words that sound alike?

Knock, knock.

Who's there?

Comma.

Comma who?

Comma little closer and I'll tell you.

Knock, knock.

Who's there?

Police.

Police who?

Police open the door.

It's freezing out here!

93

Knock, knock.

Who's there?

Lettuce.

Lettuce who?

Lettuce in, and you'll see!

What steps should you take if you see a Sasquatch on your travels?

Very **large** ones.

What room has no door, no windows, no floor, and no roof?

A mushroom!

Q Why did the chicken end up in the soup?

A Bad cluck!

Knock, knock.

Who's there?

Doughnut.

Doughnut who?

Doughnut open your door to strangers!

Q Why did the worm go to the library?

A Because it was **a bookworm!**

Knock, knock.
Who's there?
Wooden.
Wooden who?
Wooden you like to know?

If two's company and three's a crowd, what's four and five?

Nine.

Q Which two letters of the alphabet contain nothing?

A **MT**

What's at the end of a rainbow?

The letter W.

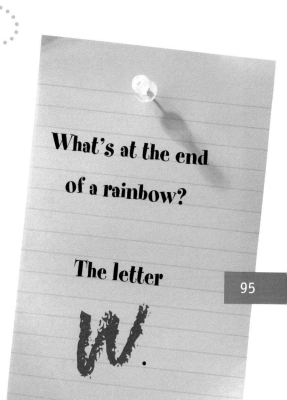

DIG DEEPER ....

1. With a partner, write a new knock-knock joke of your own.

2. Choose one of the jokes and turn it into a cartoon. You can use both thought and speech balloons.

MUTTS

by Patrick McDonnell

How can there be humour without words?

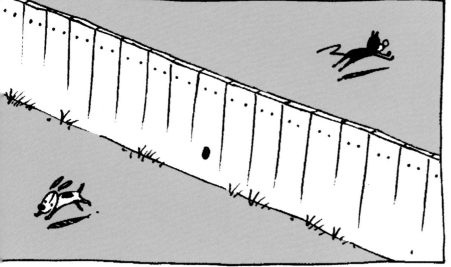

MEDIA WATCH

Find the comics page from a newspaper. What do you notice about the way the titles are printed?

DIG DEEPER

1. Make thought balloons for the cat and the dog.
2. With a partner, act out the cartoon without saying any words. Make your actions as funny as you can.

Possum's Tail

How can you learn a lesson from a funny story?

READ LIKE A WRITER

How does the author use a variety of describing words to tell about Possum's tail?

Characters

NARRATOR

BEAR

RABBIT

TURTLE

RACCOON

POSSUM

OTTER

CRICKET

Props/Scenery

- forest (a painted backdrop or potted plants)
- bandage for Possum's tail
- medicine bottle or bowl for Possum's tail
- oak tree (can be painted on a backdrop)

Costumes

Narrator: cloth turban (traditionally worn by Cherokee men)

Animals: masks made from paper plates decorated with markers, yarn, cotton balls, or beads

Possum: The furry tail can be made of stuffed socks. The rat's tail can be a piece of rope.

by Joseph Bruchac

Scene I: The Forest

A group of animals stands together.

NARRATOR: Long ago Possum had the most beautiful tail of all the animals. Everyone knew that was true. And if anyone didn't know, then Possum would tell him so.

BEAR: Tomorrow we will have a big meeting. Rabbit, you be the messenger. Go tell all the animals. We will meet at the big oak tree when Grandmother Sun rises up into the sky.

RABBIT: What will the meeting be about?

BEAR: We will decide that tomorrow.

TURTLE: Oh, no, here comes Possum!

RACCOON: He is going to brag about his tail again. I can tell.

Possum enters and walks over to the other animals, holding his long tail in front of him.

POSSUM: *Siyo!* (see-yo) Hello! This day is beautiful. And so is my tail. Look at my beautiful tail.

OTHER ANIMALS: *Siyo*, Possum.

POSSUM: Did you say there would be a meeting tomorrow?

BEAR: Yes.

POSSUM: Then I should speak at the meeting.

TURTLE: Why?

OTTER: Turtle, don't ask him! He'll just talk about his—

POSSUM: Because of my beautiful tail. It is the most beautiful of all. It is not short like Bear's tail. It is long and silky. It is not stiff like Raccoon's tail. It is soft and lovely. It is not stubby like Rabbit's tail. It is fluffy and big. It is not ugly like Turtle's tail. It is pretty and nice. *(Possum can continue to improvise while Bear and Rabbit speak, saying "Isn't it beautiful?" etc.)*

As Possum goes on talking, the other animals yawn and roll their eyes. One by one they fall to the ground and pretend to sleep.

Rabbit taps Bear on the shoulder, and Rabbit and Bear step toward the audience. Possum does not notice, but keeps talking.

RABBIT:	I have an idea about Possum.
BEAR:	We should stuff moss into our ears so we cannot hear him?
RABBIT:	No, I have a better idea than that. Let me whisper it to you.
	Rabbit whispers into Bear's ear. Bear smiles and nods.
BEAR:	That is a good idea.

Bear and Rabbit turn back toward Possum, who is still talking. The other animals are still pretending to sleep, but Possum doesn't notice.

RABBIT: Possum, you *do* have a beautiful tail.

POSSUM: Yes. That is true. Shall I tell you about it?

BEAR: No! I mean, not now.

RABBIT: We have decided that you should be the first speaker at the big meeting tomorrow.

POSSUM: Of course. That is true. The one with the most beautiful tail should always speak first.

RABBIT: Possum, your tail should look its best for the meeting.

POSSUM: Of course. That is true. My tail should look its best.

RABBIT: I will take you to Cricket. He will put some special medicine on your tail. Then your tail will be ready for the meeting.

POSSUM: Of course. That is true. Let us go to Cricket.

Possum and Rabbit go offstage together. The other animals open their eyes and sit up.

RACCOON: Oh, no!

OTTER: If Possum's tail is made more beautiful, he'll never stop talking.

TURTLE: Otter is right. We'll all have to move away to escape his bragging.

BEAR: Don't worry. Rabbit has a plan.

Scene II: Another Part of the Forest

Cricket crouches on the ground.

RABBIT: Cricket, I want you to put some of your *special* medicine on Possum's tail.

POSSUM: Yes. That is true. I want my tail to look even more beautiful.

CRICKET: Rabbit, do you mean my *special* medicine?

RABBIT: Yes, I mean your *special* medicine.

POSSUM: Hurry up. I want you to fix my tail.

CRICKET: I will fix it. *(Cricket pretends to put medicine on Possum's tail.)* This medicine will make your tail look as it has never looked before.

POSSUM: Will everyone notice it?

CRICKET: Oh yes, everyone will notice it. *(Cricket wraps a bandage around Possum's tail.)* Now you must keep this old snakeskin wrapped around your tail all night. Do not take it off until you are at the meeting.

Scene III: The Forest, Near the Big Oak Tree

All the animals are gathered in a semicircle. Possum's tail is still wrapped in the snakeskin.

BEAR: Possum will open our meeting.

RABBIT: Everyone, pay attention.

POSSUM: *Siyo*, everyone. I have been asked to speak today because of my tail. It is the most beautiful of all. Here, let me show you how beautiful it is.

Possum unwraps his tail. It now looks like a big rat's tail, but Possum does not notice.

RACCOON: Look at Possum's tail!

POSSUM: *(still showing off the tail without looking at it)* Yes. Look at my tail. Look at how beautiful it is.

TURTLE: It has no hair at all!

OTTER: It is really ugly.

RACCOON: It is funny looking.

The animals begin to laugh. Possum looks at his tail and sees that it has no hair.

POSSUM: My tail! Cricket has ruined it!

Possum sits down on the ground, closes his eyes, and then rolls onto his back with his feet up in the air. He stays there until all the other animals have gone. Then he gets up and runs away.

NARRATOR: So it is that Possum now has the ugliest tail of all the animals. Ever since that time, whenever Possum meets another animal, he closes his eyes, rolls over on his back, and pretends to be dead until the other animal goes away. And Possum no longer brags about his tail!

DIG DEEPER

1. With a group, act out all or part of the play.
2. What lesson are people supposed to learn from this play? Rewrite the ending to keep the same lesson without hurting Possum's feelings or his tail.

MEDIA WATCH

Look in newspapers and magazines for reviews of funny movies and plays.

Performers at Work!

In readers' theatre, performers read a story to the audience. They don't act it out. Each person reads a part.

It's your turn to write and perform a readers' theatre.

Plan Your Presentation

- Work with a group.
- Choose a funny story.
- Make a script showing the parts:
  - A different person reads the dialogue for each character.
  - A narrator reads the words that are not in the dialogue.
  - You can have more than one narrator.
- Make sure everyone has a part.

READERS' THEATRE

A good story for a readers' theatre:
- has lots of dialogue
- is easy to read out loud
- has interesting details
- is not too long

Practise

Practise, practise, practise!

- First, practise your parts alone.
- Then, practise together as a group.
- Record your practices and listen to them.

PERFORMANCE TIPS!

- Don't read too quickly or too slowly.
- Make sure everyone can hear you.
- Put expression in your voice.

Present Your Readers' Theatre

- Present your story to another group or to the class.
- When you are finished, invite your audience to give you feedback. Ask:
  - What questions do you have?
  - What did you like best?
  - What could we work on?
- Write a reflection in your journal.

BE A GOOD AUDIENCE!

- Sit quietly and listen.
- Show that you appreciate the performers.
- Ask questions when they are finished.

How might a fairy tale princess invent pizza?

The Princess and the Pizza

by Mary Jane and Herm Auch

Princess Paulina needed a job. Her father had given up his throne to become a wood-carver and moved them to a humble shack in a neighbouring kingdom. Since the king was still learning, his carvings didn't sell, and Paulina's garden barely kept enough on the table. Paulina missed princessing. She missed walking the peacock in the royal garden, surveying the kingdom from the castle tower, and doing the princess wave in royal processions.

Paulina tried walking a stray chicken around her shack, but it only pecked at her bare toes. Surveying the kingdom from the shack's leaky roof made even more holes. She tried princess-waving to the townspeople from her father's cart, but nobody bothered to wave back. They just thought she was swatting at flies.

READ LIKE A WRITER

Many of the important words in the title and the story start with the same sound. What effect does repeating the same sound have?

One day, a page rode past the shack, announcing that Queen Zelda of Blom was seeking a true princess to become the bride of her son, Prince Drupert.

"This is my chance to get back to princessing," Paulina cried. She rummaged through her trunk of ex-princess stuff, brushed the wood shavings from her best ball gown, and blew away the bits of sawdust that clung to her diamond tiara. Then she tucked a piece of garlic into her bodice for good luck, snipped some fragrant herbs to cover up the garlic smell, and headed for the castle.

Paulina didn't expect much competition. There wasn't another princess for hundreds of miles. But when she got to Blom Castle, Paulina found she was only one of twelve princesses hoping to become the royal bride.

When she looked into her assigned room, Paulina saw her bed piled with sixteen mattresses. "Oh, for Pete's sake. The old princess-and-the-pea trick. That's so once-upon-a-time." Naturally, Paulina didn't sleep all night because she felt the lumpy pea through all of the mattresses.

When the twelve princesses gathered in the throne room the next morning, the seven who looked bright-eyed were sent home. Now only Paulina and four other sleepy princesses remained.

First, they were made to write essays entitled "Why I Want to Have the Gracious and Exquisitely Beautiful Queen Zelda for My Mother-in-Law."

Prince Drupert and Queen Zelda finally appeared on the balcony. Queen Zelda did all the talking. "Congratulations, ladies, you have written some lovely essays, which I will keep in my scrapbook. And you have all passed the mattress test. But to make absolutely sure you are of royal blood, there is a second test. Only a true princess can wear these glass slippers."

111

"For Pete's sake, you never heard of sneakers?" Paulina asked.

Queen Zelda gave Paulina a sharp look. "Nobody said you had to hike in them. Just try them on."

After the royal page made his way around the room with the slippers, two big-footed princesses were sent home. Now only Paulina and two others remained. One was followed around by seven strange little men, and the other had such a long braid dragging behind her, Paulina kept tripping over it.

"For Pete's sake, you never heard of scissors?" Paulina cried.

Queen Zelda glared at Paulina.

"You have all passed the second princess test. Your final task is to cook a feast that proves you worthy of being my dear Drupert's wife."

This set up a wail among the princesses, especially Paulina. "For Pete's sake. You have no royal chef?"

"Silence!" said the queen. "The table holds the makings for three fine feasts. Choose well, for the winner will become my dear Drupert's bride."

As Paulina started for the table, the long-haired princess tripped her, then loaded up with food. By the time Paulina got there, the seven strange little men had run off with everything but some flour, yeast, water, three overripe tomatoes, and a hunk of stale cheese.

"Hey, that's not fair! Queen Zelda, will you help me?"

"No," said the queen. "Because you have a big mouth."

A servant escorted Paulina to her room and locked the door. "Hey! How can I cook without a bowl or spoons or pots?"

There was no reply.

Paulina tried to make bread, kneading the flour, water, and yeast together; but it only stuck to the tray in a flattened mess. She squished the tomatoes over the dough to brighten it up. It looked awful. She sprinkled cheese gratings over the top. It was still a mess, and Paulina was exhausted.

"For Pete's sake, where's your fairy godmother when you need her? I'm going to take a nap." She reached under the pile of mattresses, pulled out the offending pea, and climbed into bed. She hadn't been sleeping long when there was knock at the door.

"Only twenty minutes left," called Queen Zelda. "I don't smell anything cooking."

"I'm not cooking," said Paulina. "I'm napping. Then I'm going home."

"You're not going anywhere," said the queen. "The losers will be beheaded."

Paulina sat bolt upright. "Beheaded! You didn't tell us that!"

"I forgot," said the queen.

"Can't I have a second chance? How about I try to spin straw into gold? Or maybe I could guess a weird little man's name?"

"No second chances," declared the queen.

"But that's not fair!" Paulina cried.

"Who needs to be fair? I'm the queen."

Paulina leaped out of bed and ran to the window, but it was an unbelievably long drop to the ground. The meal was her only hope. She rushed the tray over to the fireplace, stirred the few remaining hot coals, then crushed her garlic and sprinkled it over the mess for good luck. Finally, Paulina tossed on the herbs to cover up the garlic smell.

Paulina paced back and forth, planning her escape. Perhaps she could make a deal with the long-haired princess to climb down her braid. She didn't notice that the goopy dough had browned into a crust, the tomatoes were bubbling, the hard bits of cheese had melted, and the fragrance of garlic and herbs filled the room.

A page opened the door. "Time's up."

Paulina took a deep breath and carried her tray into the great dining room.

The other princesses had made lovely feasts, especially the one who had the seven strange little men to help her.

Prince Drupert went right to Paulina's tray. "It's not pretty, but it smells scrumptious." He helped himself to an unusually generous piece. "What do you call this dish?"

Paulina shrugged. "I don't know."

"It can't be an official entry in the contest if it doesn't have a name," said the queen.

"Oh, for Pete's sake," Paulina muttered.

"What's that?" snapped the queen. "Pete's what?"

Remembering the beheading threat, Paulina frantically tried to think of a name. "It's Pete's...ah..."

"Pizza?" The queen took a big bite. "Odd name, but it's tasty. The winner is Paulina's pizza."

"You mean I won't be beheaded?"

"I was only kidding about the beheading," said the queen.

"Then I was only kidding about wanting to marry Prince Drupert. Who needs him? I have other plans."

"Will you leave your recipe?" asked the queen.

"No way," said Paulina. "It's just become a family secret." She headed for the door.

"I liked you best," whined the queen, following close behind.

"Oh, for Pete's sake," muttered Paulina as she stomped across the drawbridge.

Princess Paulina's Pizza Palace opened a few weeks later. It featured unusual, carved furniture and fifty kinds of pizza.

Every Thursday, on the royal chef's night off, Queen Zelda and Prince Drupert came to Paulina's for popcorn-pineapple pizza. They often stayed to play cards with Paulina's father.

From then on, whenever Paulina drove her pizza delivery cart through town doing the princess wave, everybody waved back and ran after her, asking about the day's specials.

Life was good. Paulina was grateful not to have Queen Zelda for a mother-in-law, but she still worried about one little thing.

She worried about getting Queen Zelda as her stepmother!

DIG DEEPER ....

1. Imagine you are Prince Drupert. Write a diary entry in which you tell about the contest and Princess Paulina's pizza.

2. With a group, create a TV commercial for Princess Paulina's Pizza Palace.

MEDIA WATCH

With a group, make a list of the fairy tale princesses you have seen in movies.

Connect and Share

People everywhere enjoy sharing funny stories. Friends, families, and classmates often retell stories they have heard. One way to share stories is in a cartoon.

Now it's your turn to share!

Take a story home!

- Choose a story from this unit or make up your own.
- Draw four cartoon panels showing what happened.
- Put in speech balloons but leave them empty.
- Take your cartoon story home.

Bring a story back!

- Show your cartoon story to family members.
- Have them help you fill in the speech balloons.
- Bring the cartoon back to school to share with your classmates.

CARTOONING TIPS

- Choose the most important parts.
- Have a beginning, middle, and end.
- Let the pictures tell the story.
- Think like a character when you write speech balloons and thought balloons.

Spotlight on Learning

Collect

■ Gather your notebooks, writing, cartoons, and other media work you did in this unit. Include planning notes and reflections for oral activities.

Talk and reflect

Work with a partner.

■ Together, read the Learning Goals on page 62.

■ Talk about how well you met these goals.

■ Look through your work for evidence.

Select

■ Choose two pieces of work that show how you achieved the Learning Goals. (The same piece of work can show more than one goal.)

Tell about your choices

■ Tell what each piece shows about your learning.

My choices	I want this in my portfolio because...

Reflect

■ What have you learned about reading, listening to, and viewing funny stories?

■ What have you learned about creating them?

■ What was one of your favourite stories? What made you like it?

119

Amazing Places!

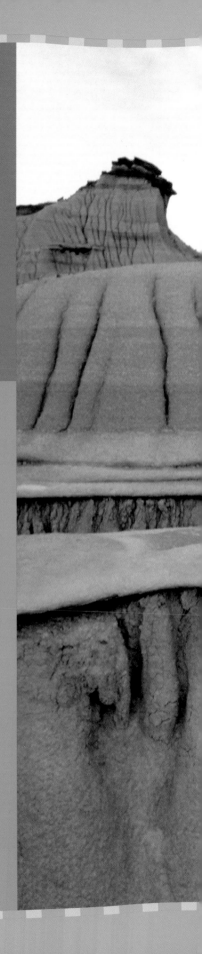

LEARNING GOALS

In this unit you will:

- Read, view, and listen to information about interesting places in Canada.

- Record and organize important information and ideas you learn.

- Write, illustrate, and share facts about amazing places.

- Use speaking strategies and skills when you present to an audience.

protected parks
national
landforms
preservation
buried treasures
roadside attractions

121

Drumheller Dinosaur Dance

by Robert Heidbreder

Illustrated by Bill Slavin
and Esperança Melo

Where would you go to see a dinosaur dance?

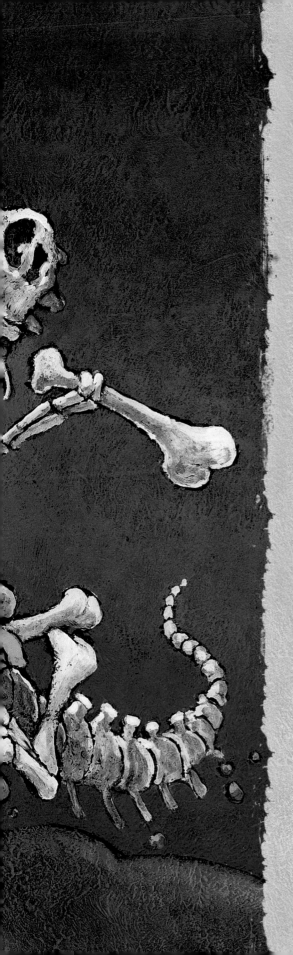

Drumheller dinosaurs lie around,
bones buried deep in ancient ground.

Dry bones rest in dusty sleep—
skulls, claws, jaws down dinosaur deep.

Drumheller dinosaurs make no noise.
All day they're as silent as dinosaur toys.

But when the moon rises in the sky,
Drumheller dinosaurs transmogrify.

They stir their bones from secret cracks
and assemble themselves—fronts, sides and backs.

Drumheller dinosaurs rise up tall.
Across the Badlands they skeleton-crawl.

They creep to a spot that they all know.
They band together, ROAR 1-2-3 GO!

They grab buried drums and begin a beat.
They rattle, clack, stomp on dinosaur feet.

BOOMITY-BOOM RATTELY-CLACK
THUMPITY-THUMP WHICKETY-WHACK

Cymbals crash, stone castanets snap.
They dance back to life with a clickity-clap.

BOOMITY-BOOM RATTELY-CLACK
THUMPITY-THUMP WHICKETY-WHACK

123

They tango, fandango and break-dance with ease.
They whirl on their tails and twirl on their knees.

BOOMITY-BOOM RATTELY-CLACK
THUMPITY-THUMP WHICKETY-WHACK

With wild tambourines they shimmy and shake.
They rock and they roll—it's a dino earthquake!

BOOMITY-BOOM RATTELY-CLACK
THUMPITY-THUMP WHICKETY-WHACK

The thunderous beat rolls into town.
Sleep is disturbed for miles around.

"A terrible storm!" the grown-ups shout.
But the kids all know that the dinos are out.

The dinosaurs' party is loud and long,
with drumming and dancing and Drumheller song.

BOOMITY-BOOM RATTELY-CLACK
THUMPITY-THUMP WHICKETY-WHACK

The kids go to sleep to the dinosaur beat.
They bob their heads and tip-tap their feet.

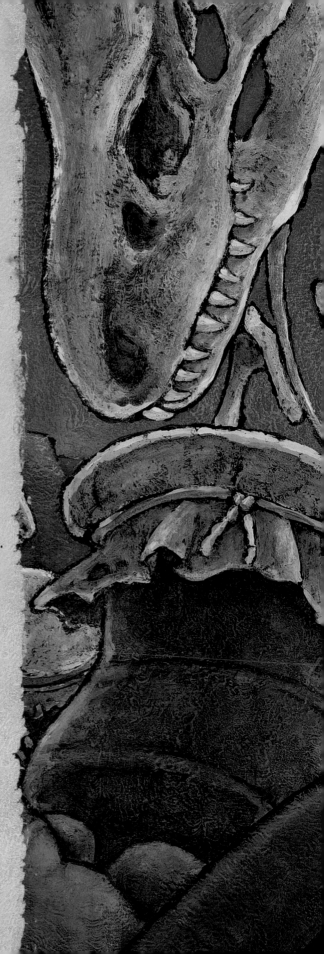

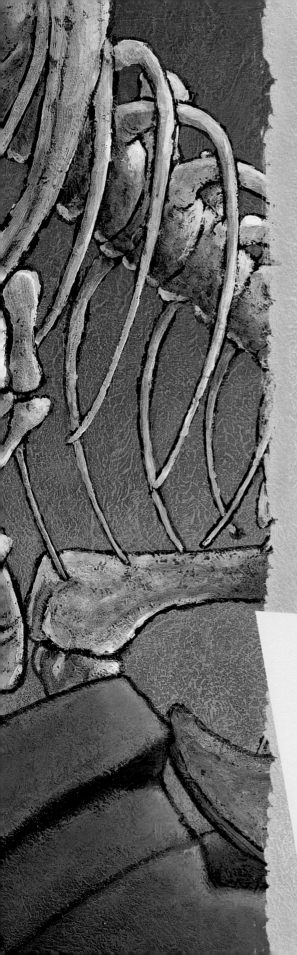

They dance in their dreams with wiggles and jiggles,
smiles on their faces and mouths full of giggles.

But when dark night gives way to the day,
Drumheller dinosaurs stash drums away.

Then off they clatter through dinosaur land,
keeping the beat of their Drumheller band.

BOOMITY-BOOM RATTELY-CLACK
THUMPITY-THUMP WHICKETY-WHACK

Across the Badlands they creep to their beds,
unsnap tired bones and bury sleepy heads.

They're deep in the earth
by dawn's first light,
where they wait all day long
for dinosaur night.

LET'S TALK ABOUT IT...

- What makes the Badlands a good place for a dinosaur dance?
- What would be a good way to present this poem to an audience? Choose a part of the poem and perform it.

Reading in Social Studies

Reading in social studies helps you to learn about people and places in our world. Think of an interesting place in Canada.

- How did you learn about this place?
- What is it like?
- What interests you about it?

TALK ABOUT IT!

- Tell a partner about your interesting place.
- How can you learn more about this and other places?

Here are some clues.

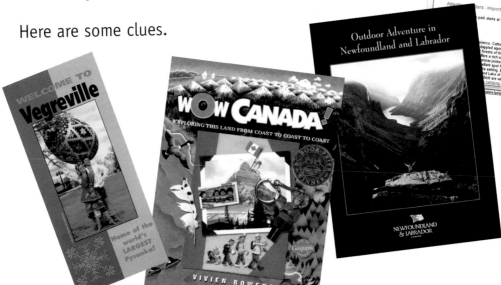

Make a chart together.

Learning About Places	
Where you can find out	Examples

Think Like a Reader

Here it is!
A landform is a
feature on the
earth's surface.

Read with a purpose

■ Why do you look for information about places?

Crack the code

Use a dictionary to help you read and understand difficult words. Keep a list of new words.

Make meaning

Practise using these strategies when you read social studies information:

USE WHAT YOU KNOW
Look at the visuals and the headings. What do they make you think of?

DECIDE WHAT'S IMPORTANT
As you read, pick out important information.

SUMMARIZE
Organize the information in a chart or a web.

Analyze what you read

■ How can you check whether the facts you read are correct?

■ Why might two people tell about the same place in a different way?

Fathom Five

National Marine Park

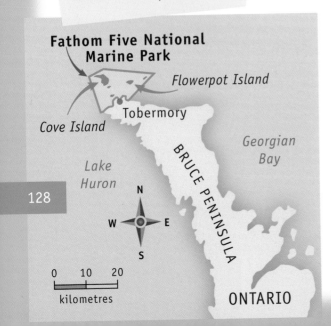

Fathom Five National Marine Park

Flowerpot Island

Tobermory

Cove Island

Georgian Bay

Lake Huron

BRUCE PENINSULA

N
W E
S

0 10 20
kilometres

ONTARIO

128

A Water Park

Fathom Five National Marine Park is different from other parks in Canada. Most of it is under water! It has 20 different islands and 22 old shipwrecks. Fathom Five is one of the best places to scuba dive in North America.

Location

This park is in southern Ontario at the tip of the Bruce Peninsula. Tobermory is the nearest town. Divers can rent gear there. Visitors may also choose to cruise through the park in glass-bottom tour boats.

Nature

Fathom Five is a great place to enjoy nature. There are many caves and rocky cliffs to explore. People interested in plants can find all kinds of rare ferns, orchids, and trees that are a thousand years old.

The wildlife on each island is quite different. Cove Island has deer, black bears, and rattlesnakes. On Flowerpot Island there are garter snakes and red squirrels. Visitors can watch loons diving for fish. It is even possible to see a turtle or an otter.

Origin

In 1972, the Canadian government declared Fathom Five a provincial marine park. A university student had come up with the idea. It became Canada's first national marine park in 1987. Since then, it has been a model for other marine parks.

Visitors enjoy scuba diving, snorkelling, boating, camping, and hiking. Some people explore caves too.

DECIDE WHAT'S IMPORTANT
What are the key points about this park?

One of the "flowerpots" on Flowerpot Island.

SUMMARIZE
Organize the information in a web.

Roosevelt Campobello International Park

The "Sunsweep" sculpture honours the friendship between Canada and the U.S. One arched stone sits in this park. The other is on the west coast. Together they form an imaginary arch along the Canada/U.S. border.

130

USE WHAT YOU KNOW

What do you think an international park is?

An Island Park

Roosevelt Campobello International Park is on an island off the coast of New Brunswick. Former U.S. President F.D. Roosevelt spent many vacations there. Today, visitors can tour the historical buildings. They can enjoy the formal gardens or hike in the wilderness areas. This park is a great place to watch the tides. The ocean views are amazing. There are pebbly beaches, foggy forests, and rugged cliffs to explore.

Location

The park is in the south part of Campobello Island on the Bay of Fundy. This island is part of New Brunswick but is very close to Maine in the United States. A ferry runs from the New Brunswick mainland to Deer Island. A second ferry goes from there to Campobello Island.

Wildlife

Many red squirrels and snowshoe hares live in this island park. Beaver, white-tailed deer, moose, bobcats, black bears, coyotes, and weasels also make their homes there. Visitors can hear fin whales, mink whales, or humpback whales blowing air as they rise to the water's surface. Porpoises, dolphins, and harbour seals can be seen from along the shore.

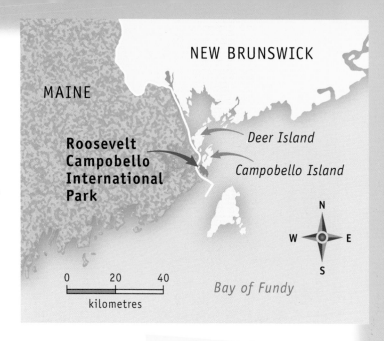

Origins

The park was established in 1964. The Prime Minister of Canada, Lester B. Pearson, and President Lyndon B. Johnson, the president of the United States, signed the agreement. Unlike any other park in the world, the two nations manage the park together and share the cost.

Today, visitors enjoy whale watching, hiking, bird watching, and picnicking.

DECIDE WHAT'S IMPORTANT

What are the key points about this park?

SUMMARIZE

Organize the information in a web.

131

Khutzeymateen Grizzly Sanctuary

An Untouched Wilderness

Khutzeymateen (KOOT-sa mateen) is a wilderness sanctuary. It was established to protect grizzly bears. There are no roads, campsites, or buildings in this park. The old-growth rainforests are full of Sitka spruce trees. The water in the rivers and fiords is clear and clean.

Location

The Khutzeymateen Grizzly Sanctuary is on the north coast of British Columbia. It is 40 kilometres northeast of Prince Rupert. Only 180 visitors may visit this park each year. Visitors must travel with a licensed guide on a chartered boat. From the boats they try to spot the grizzlies on the shore.

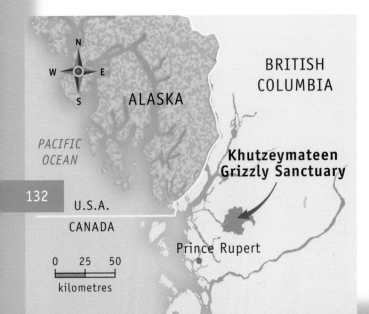

BRITISH COLUMBIA

ALASKA

PACIFIC OCEAN

Khutzeymateen Grizzly Sanctuary

U.S.A.
CANADA

Prince Rupert

0   25   50
kilometres

132

Wildlife

About 50 grizzly bears live in this large valley. It is sometimes called the "Garden of the Grizzlies." In this sanctuary all grizzly bears are protected. They cannot be hunted. In late summer, the bears can have a feast. At that time, salmon, the bears' favourite food, come to the rivers to spawn.

Moose, wolves, black bears, and over 100 species of birds also live in the park. The rivers and inlets are home to beavers, otters, harbour seals, orcas, and humpback whales.

DECIDE WHAT'S IMPORTANT
What are the key points about this sanctuary?

A mother grizzly plays with her cubs, but is always on the lookout for danger.

Origin

The Tsimshian (Sim-she-an) Gitsee are a First Nations people who used to fish and hunt in this valley. They still live in this region along with other First Nations people. The Khutzeymateen Grizzly Sanctuary was created in 1994. The government of British Columbia and the Tsimshian Gitsee people now co-manage the park.

Only a few lucky people are allowed to view this park. This lets the bears live undisturbed in the wild.

Bear Fact

The greatest threat to bears is loss of habitat. Before the Europeans came to North America, there were about 200 000 grizzly bears. Today, there are only about 25 000.

SUMMARIZE
Organize the information in a web.

Reflect on Your Reading

You have ...

- talked about special places in Canada.
- read reports to learn about protected parks.
- learned new words that describe some parks.

national heritage extraordinary
preservation fathom
international peninsula

I worry that too many visitors may spoil the protected parks. Do you think that's possible?

USE WHAT YOU KNOW

DECIDE WHAT'S IMPORTANT

SUMMARIZE

You have also ...

- explored different reading strategies.

Write About Learning

Which strategy did you find most helpful in reading one of the reports from "Protected Parks"? Explain how you used it. How will this strategy help in reading other reports in social studies?

Read Like a Writer

When you were reading "Protected Parks," you were reading *reports*. People read reports to get information about a specific topic.

TALK ABOUT IT!

- What do you notice about the way reports are written?
- Make a chart to list features often used in a report.

HINT!

Think about the **organization** of the reports.

Reports
- are usually written in paragraphs
- start by telling what the report is about
- give interesting details
- end with a sentence that sums up the main ideas
- include features such as charts, maps, and photos

135

Super Sand!

by Laura Langston

Each year, about 40 000 people come to admire the fantastic sand sculptures at Harrison Hot Springs.

How could sand make a place special?

Every year, the beach at Harrison Hot Springs, British Columbia, turns into a giant outdoor art gallery. That's when the World Championship Sand Sculpture Competition is held. People come from across Canada and around the world to compete. They work to sculpt sand into many different shapes, including castles, dragons, giants, and ships.

The contest is open only to master sculptors with years of experience. Some of the sculptors have carved with sand before. Others have carved with wood, metal, or marble. Some people work in teams, while others work alone. They spend days creating their masterpieces. It is hard, heavy work.

The contest starts every year after Labour Day. Judging takes place six days later. The finished sculptures stay on the beach until Thanksgiving Day. There are at least 50 sculptures created every year.

136

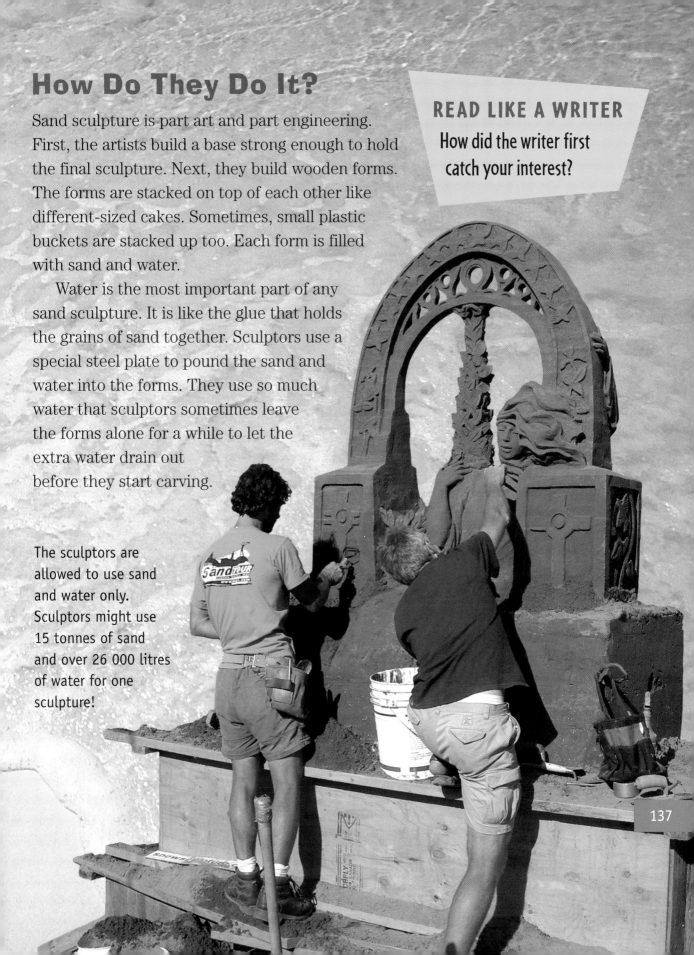

How Do They Do It?

Sand sculpture is part art and part engineering. First, the artists build a base strong enough to hold the final sculpture. Next, they build wooden forms. The forms are stacked on top of each other like different-sized cakes. Sometimes, small plastic buckets are stacked up too. Each form is filled with sand and water.

Water is the most important part of any sand sculpture. It is like the glue that holds the grains of sand together. Sculptors use a special steel plate to pound the sand and water into the forms. They use so much water that sculptors sometimes leave the forms alone for a while to let the extra water drain out before they start carving.

The sculptors are allowed to use sand and water only. Sculptors might use 15 tonnes of sand and over 26 000 litres of water for one sculpture!

READ LIKE A WRITER
How did the writer first catch your interest?

137

When the forms are ready, sculptors climb them like a set of stairs. They remove the wood from the top form and carve the sand. Then they step down and do the same thing to the level below. They keep going until they are done.

Rain is good for sand sculptures. Even heavy rain makes them stronger. Hot, dry wind is the enemy. It sucks moisture from the sculptures and steals grains of sand. This is a process called erosion.

Canada is a sandy place. There are sand dunes in every province and territory. They were created thousands of years after the last Ice Age. Sand dunes provide an important habitat for birds, rodents, and plants. Coastal sand dunes protect our shorelines.

Finished sculptures are sprayed with a special product that helps them to last longer.

EVERYBODY IS A WINNER

It's All About the Sand!

Not all sand is the same. Ocean sand is round because it rolls with the tide for hundreds of years. It is also salty, and mixed with shells and seaweed. The sand at Harrison comes from the bottom of Harrison Lake. It was deposited there during the last Ice Age. It has sharp corners and is mixed with dirt. When water is added, it sticks together much better than ocean sand.

People come to Harrison Lake to see the sand sculpture competition. Visitors come from around the world to soak in the hot springs. But they can also go hiking, fishing, and bird watching. The surrounding area is home to wintering eagles, snow geese, and beautiful trumpeter swans. All these things combine to make the Harrison Lake area one amazing place!

Harrison Lake is a popular place for boating and swimming.

MEDIA WATCH

Look in tourism brochures or on the Internet to find out about other sand and ice sculpture contests.

DIG DEEPER

1. Make a list or web showing reasons why the Harrison Lake area is a good place for the sand sculpture competition.

2. Imagine yourself as a master sculptor in the competition. Draw what you would create. List the basic steps you'd follow in creating a sculpture.

Harrison Lake

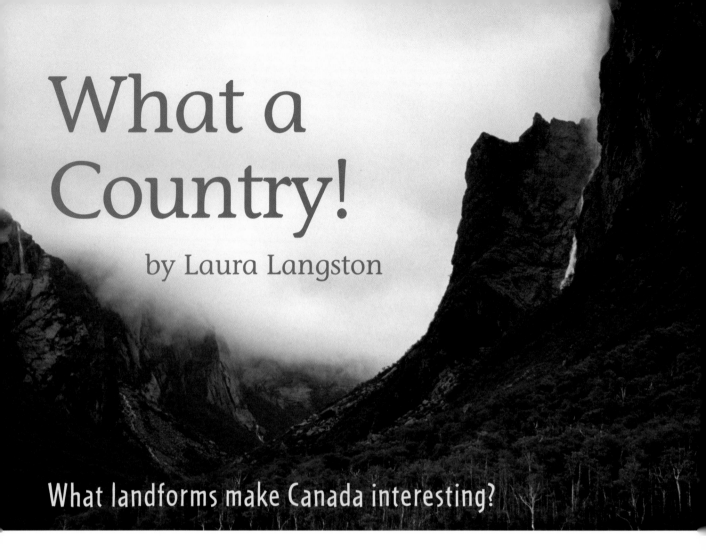

What a Country!

by Laura Langston

What landforms make Canada interesting?

Gros Morne National Park is on the west coast of Newfoundland.

The Ancient Mountains of Gros Morne

The mountains of Gros Morne National Park can teach us about how Earth has changed. Millions of years ago, parts of Earth collided. This caused folds of land to push up from deep inside the planet and from the bottom of the sea. These folds formed mountains. If you hike through Gros Morne, you could walk on what once was a beach or an ocean floor.

Part of the Long Range Mountains is in Gros Morne Park. This mountain range was once as high as the Rocky Mountains in Western Canada. Over time, the Long Range Mountains have been worn down by wind, water, and ice.

The Natural Wonder of Niagara Falls

Niagara Falls is over 12 000 years old. Back then, southern Ontario was covered in a layer of ice two or three kilometres thick. As the ice melted, it carved out the Great Lakes. The water spilled out of what is now Lake Erie. It ran downhill towards Lake Ontario and wore a path as it went. This became the Niagara River. At one place the riverbed dropped steeply, like an underwater cliff. This formed Niagara Falls.

Niagara Falls is part of the Niagara Escarpment. An escarpment is a natural slope or steep cliff. The Niagara Escarpment stretches from Tobermory in the north to Niagara Falls in the south. Its rocks are more than 400 million years old. The Niagara Escarpment has been declared a protected area and the Falls are considered one of the world's great natural wonders.

Niagara Falls is 52 metres high. It is not the world's tallest waterfall, but it has some of the fastest flowing rapids. Water going over the falls travels about 69 kilometres an hour.

READ LIKE A WRITER

Why does the writer use headings to help her readers?

Did You Know...?

The roar of Niagara Falls is the sound of air bubbles breaking as they are slammed out of the water.

Canada's Rainforest

Rainforests are warm and always wet. They are very important to our planet. They are home to millions of plants and animals. The plants make much of Earth's oxygen. Rainforests also recycle and clean water.

Rainforests are not just found in the tropics. There is a temperate rainforest on the west coast of North America. It starts in Northern California and goes all the way up to Glacier Bay in Alaska. One of the largest, undisturbed pieces of that forest is in British Columbia. It is called the Great Bear Rainforest.

First Nations peoples have lived in this forest for centuries. It has lakes, waterfalls, and many different kinds of plants and animals. Grizzly bears, black bears, and Kermode bears live there.

Kermode bears are also called Spirit Bears. In 2006, the Spirit Bear was made the official provincial mammal of British Columbia.

A Kermode bear walks with her two black cubs in the Great Bear Rainforest. The forest lies between the northern tip of Vancouver Island and the Alaska border.

Magnificent Hoodoos of the Badlands

Hoodoos can be the height of an average person or they can be taller than a 10-storey building.

Hoodoos are tall, skinny rocks that come in fantastic shapes. Some look like mushrooms. Others look like strange pillars with windows. These rocks are found in dry areas, such as the Badlands of Alberta. Hoodoos formed as the Ice Age ended, about 10 000 years ago.

Hoodoos are made up of many layers of soft sandstone. A long time ago, the sandstone mixed with harder rock. As a result, some parts of the hoodoo are harder than others. Over the years, wind, rain, and freezing temperatures slowly eroded or wore away some of the sandstone, leaving the harder rock behind.

DIG DEEPER

1. Make a Venn Diagram comparing two of the places in this selection.

2. Think of interesting features of the land in your area or in a place you have visited. Make a poster to convince tourists to visit it. Include a coloured photo or drawing, and points to describe it.

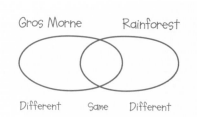

Writers at Work!

It's your turn to be an author and illustrator. Make a picture book for Grade Ones about places in Canada.

Plan Your Book

- Choose a place or places in Canada that a Grade One child would find interesting.
- Make a web of the features of books you liked in Grade One.
- Ask a librarian to show you some non-fiction books for young children.
- In a small group, think about what type of book will work well—a big book, small book, or pop-up book?

IDEAS TO TRY

- Talk to Grade Ones about their interests.
- Select places from the Internet, this book, or magazines.
- Think about places that you liked when you were in Grade One.

Create the Pages

With a group or on your own:

- Plan the pages of your book.
- Begin to draw and write, perhaps using a computer program.

THINGS TO REMEMBER

- Make a cover and a title page.
- Create large, bright pictures.
- Write a short sentence to tell about each picture.

Think About Changes

- Will your book be interesting to a Grade One child?
- Do your illustrations and text go together?
- How can you improve your work?

Check It Over

- Do your sentences have capitals and correct punctuation?
- Are words spelled correctly?
- Are your illustrations carefully done?
- Make your changes and get ready to publish.

Share Your Book

- Think of how you will present your published copy.

WAYS TO SHARE

- Read your book to Grade One children and talk about it.
- Give your book to a Grade One classroom.
- Make an e-book copy for the library.

Buried Treasures by Tina Holdcroft

What is interesting about these two places?

READ LIKE A WRITER

How does the writer show the order of events?

Gold Rush!

Come along with me.

Gold!

Gold! On August 16, 1896, gold is discovered right here, near the Klondike and Yukon Rivers. Lucky people living nearby hear the news first and rush in to claim some good gold mining land.

The ones who strike it rich pack up their gold and sail south the following spring.

About 100 000 gold seekers rush north in 1897–98. Here's one way to get to the gold—first take a steamship to Alaska then start the twisting 1000 km trek to the Klondike with a staggering climb up the Chilkoot Mountain Pass.

BORDER
ALASKA : YUKON
U.S.A □ CANADA

February 1898

Is your backpack heavy? It's time to climb up 1200 steep stairs cut into the winter ice on Chilkoot Pass. Don't step out of line. No one will let you back in. Are you tired? Too bad. It takes about 30 trips to get all of your supplies to the top.

Groan

Gasp

Grunt

Grimace

Grumble

Gulp

I'm filthy rich!

Sorry—you can't enter Canada without food and supplies to last a year.

This rule prevents a disaster! Even so, lots of gold seekers freeze to death and many more lose fingers and toes to frostbite.

April 1898

Finally, you reach the first of the lakes and rivers that lead to the Klondike. Now build yourself a raft. You're going to need one when the ice melts.

June 1898

You and 7000 boats reach the Klondike just as steamships arrive from a different route. Now where's the gold? The treasure hides deep under wet marshland and gravel, so wait for the winter freeze before you tunnel down. With luck, you'll find a layer of gold and dirt, or "paydirt."

Winter 1898–99

This lucky miner gets his gold, but what about the others? Of the 100 000 people who rush north in 1897–98, just a third reach the Klondike only to discover that all the good gold land was claimed two winters ago. By August 1899, the gold rush is over. How much treasure came out of the Klondike in the gold rush years? No one bothered to count, but in today's money it must have been a billion dollars worth of gold! What a rush!

How rich are you? Find out. Put some paydirt in a pan. Add water, tilt, and swirl. The light stuff floats and pours out, leaving the gold in the pan.

frozen muck

frozen gravel

paydirt!

bedrock

Oak Island Money Pit

In 1795, 16-year-old Daniel McGinnis sees a strange sight. An old ship's pulley, tied to a tree, dangles over a dent in the earth below. Can this mean something heavy was lowered into the ground with the pulley, then buried? Can it be the pirate treasure of Captain Kidd?

They'll need pots of money to dig out this pit!

Daniel rushes off to get two friends and some shovels. The boys soon find a layer of stones covering a pit, then deeper down they discover three oak log platforms.

I'm tired.

Let's take a break.

How about an 8-year break? We'll meet under this tree around 1803.

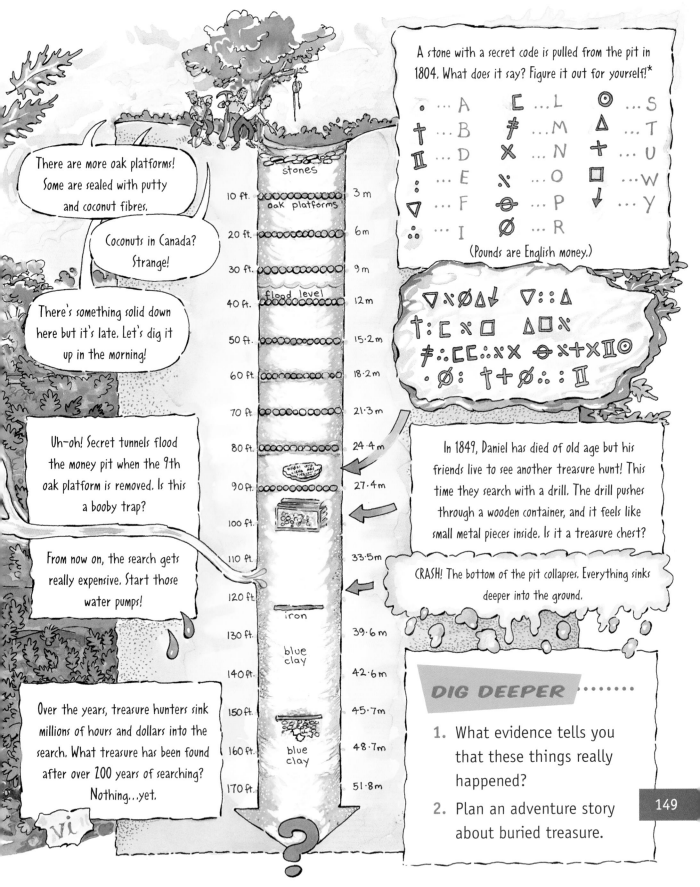

A stone with a secret code is pulled from the pit in 1804. What does it say? Figure it out for yourself!*

· ...A	⊏ ...L	⊙ ...S	
† ...B	‡ ...M	△ ...T	
Ⅱ ...D	✕ ...N	✚ ...U	
⦂ ...E	⁙ ...O	▢ ...W	
▽ ...F	⊖ ...P	↓ ...Y	
∴ ...I	∅ ...R		

(Pounds are English money.)

▽✕∅△↓ ▽∴∴△
†⦂⊏✕▢▢▢ △▢✕
‡∴⊏⊏∴✕✕ ⊖✕✚✕Ⅱ⊙
·∅ †✚∅∴∴ Ⅱ

stones

10 ft. oak platforms 3 m
20 ft. 6 m
30 ft. 9 m
flood level
40 ft. 12 m
50 ft. 15·2 m
60 ft. 18·2 m
70 ft. 21·3 m
80 ft. 24·4 m
90 ft. 27·4 m
100 ft.
110 ft. 33·5 m
120 ft.
iron
130 ft. 39·6 m
blue clay
140 ft. 42·6 m
150 ft. 45·7 m
160 ft. 48·7 m
blue clay
170 ft. 51·8 m

There are more oak platforms! Some are sealed with putty and coconut fibres.

Coconuts in Canada? Strange!

There's something solid down here but it's late. Let's dig it up in the morning!

Uh-oh! Secret tunnels flood the money pit when the 9th oak platform is removed. Is this a booby trap?

From now on, the search gets really expensive. Start those water pumps!

Over the years, treasure hunters sink millions of hours and dollars into the search. What treasure has been found after over 200 years of searching? Nothing...yet.

In 1849, Daniel has died of old age but his friends live to see another treasure hunt! This time they search with a drill. The drill pushes through a wooden container, and it feels like small metal pieces inside. Is it a treasure chest?

CRASH! The bottom of the pit collapses. Everything sinks deeper into the ground.

DIG DEEPER ·······

1. What evidence tells you that these things really happened?

2. Plan an adventure story about buried treasure.

*The answer to the riddle is: Forty feet below, two million pounds are buried.

Molly Lamb Bobak

Skaters on the Rideau, 1980

How can artists show their feelings for the places they paint?

DIG DEEPER ···········

1. Choose a piece of music to go with this painting. Present and explain your choice.

2. Paint or draw a picture of an outdoor activity in your community. Show how you feel about the place you choose.

Something to

READ LIKE A WRITER

How does the songwriter organize his ideas in this song?

152

Sing About by Oscar Brand

What does this song tell about Canada?

1 I have walked 'cross the sand on the Grand Banks of Newfoundland,
Lazed on the ridge of the Miramichi,
Seen the waves tear and roar at the stone coast of Labrador,
Watched them roll back to the great northern sea.

Refrain

From the Vancouver Island to the Alberta Highland,
'Cross the prairie, the Lakes to Ontario's towers.
From the sound of Mount Royal's chimes out to the Maritimes,
Something to Sing About, this land of ours.

2 I have welcomed the dawn from the fields of Saskatchewan,
Followed the sun to the Vancouver shore.
Watched it climb shiny new up the snow peaks of Cariboo,
Up to the clouds where the wild Rockies soar.

Refrain

DIG DEEPER

1. On a map of Canada, locate the places noted in the song.
2. Which part of the song gives you the clearest picture in your mind?

A Great Canadiar

Come along on a road trip across Canada.
In each province and territory, we'll stop to
view a large roadside attraction.

What would you expect to see
on a Great Canadian Road Trip?

Road Trip!

by Lynn Bryan

Newfoundland and Labrador

Glover's Harbour displays a life-sized copy of the World's Largest Giant Squid. It was caught near here in 1878. It measured 16.8 metres long, and had eyes as big as volleyballs! No wonder people thought it was a sea monster!

World's Largest Giant Squid, Glover's Harbour, NL

READ LIKE A WRITER

What information does the writer include in the first sentence of each section?

Nova Scotia

Marvin the Mastodon tells of a discovery that made the town of Stewiacke famous. In 1991, a backhoe operator dug up something long and white. Surprise—it was the tusk of a mastodon, an extinct Ice Age animal!

Marvin the Mastodon, Stewiacke, NS

New Brunswick

Next we check out the Giant Magnet in Moncton. It's there to catch tourists' attention and lead them to Magnetic Hill. At the bottom of the hill, they can put their car in neutral and coast uphill! Impossible? Yes, but the tilt of the land creates that feeling.

Giant Magnet, Moncton, NB

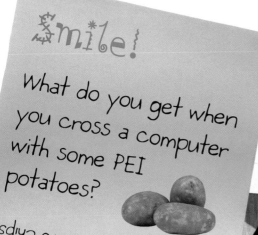

smile!

What do you get when you cross a computer with some PEI potatoes?

Micro chips.

Prince Edward Island

In the village of O'Leary we visit Canada's only potato museum. Right in front stands their Giant Potato. Did you know that farmers in PEI have been growing potatoes for the world for over 300 years?

Giant Potato, O'Leary, PE

Confederation Bridge

The Confederation Bridge joins Prince Edward Island to the rest of Canada. It's the longest bridge in the world over frozen sea.

Quebec

Now we're on the Magdalen Islands, in the Gulf of St. Lawrence. This statue honours people in the fishing industry, which is the main activity on the islands. Be sure to try some delicious seafood while you're here!

Fishermen Statue, Magdalen Islands, QC

Ontario

Here's a nickel you can't spend! It's Sudbury's Giant Canadian Nickel. Sudbury has the world's largest known deposit of nickel. This 1951 coin marks the 200th anniversary of nickel being separated from other minerals so it could be used.

Giant Nickel, Sudbury, ON

CANADA NICKEL 1751-1951 5 CENTS

Manitoba

Now, what would a camel be doing in Manitoba? Sara the Camel has become the symbol of the Spirit Sands, which are near Glenboro. This area has wind-patterned sand, cacti, and high temperatures, so it's much like a desert.

Sara the Camel, Glenboro, MB

Saskatchewan

The World's Largest Oil Can honours Ernie Symons. He produced the best squirting oil can in the world. His factory made Rocanville the "Oil Can Capital of the World." How much oil do you think this 7-metre-high oil can could hold?

The hottest temperature in Canada was recorded in Midale, SK, in July, 1937.

Symons Oil Can, Rocanville, SK

UFO Landing Pad, St. Paul, AB

Alberta

If any UFO needs to land, St. Paul has the spot! As a fun project for Canada's Centennial, the town built the World's First UFO Landing Pad. One interesting feature is a map of Canada made with stones from each province.

British Columbia

What could be more fun than jumping into the World's Largest Bathtub in Nanaimo and taking part in the yearly bathtub race? This ocean race is part of a four-day fun-filled festival that is now known worldwide.

Six Kwakwaka'wakw artists carved the World's Tallest Totem Pole that stands in Alert Bay, BC.

World's Largest Bathtub, Nanaimo, BC

Yukon Territory

Back in the Gold Rush days, Burwash Landing was a supply town for miners. So, why visit now? Perhaps to see the Largest Gold Pan in the World. On the pan is a painting of beautiful Kluane Lake, the largest lake in the Yukon.

Largest Gold Pan in the World, Burwash Landing, YT

The coldest temperature ever recorded in Canada was in Snag, Yukon. It was -63°C in February, 1947.

Northwest Territories

This marker tells travellers on the way to Inuvik that they have reached the Arctic Circle. Located on the Dempster Highway, it overlooks a beautiful view of tundra and mountains—a perfect setting for taking photos.

Arctic Circle Sign, near Fort McPherson, NT

Nunavut

Our final roadside attraction is the gigantic rock inuksuk at Rankin Inlet. An inuksuk serves as a signpost to help guide the Inuit across the treeless tundra of the Arctic. You sure can see this one from a distance!

*Inuksuk,
Rankin Inlet, NU*

Nunavut and the Northwest Territories both have license plates in the shape of a polar bear.

DIG DEEPER

1. Make a chart about the roadside attractions.
2. Why do you think communities build roadside attractions? Think about the reasons, then use them to design a roadside attraction for your community.

Attraction	Place	Why it's special

Maiden of the Mist

A LEGEND OF NIAGARA FALLS

Retold and Illustrated by Veronika Martenova Charles

Why do people tell legends?

Long ago, a Seneca tribe lived beside the Niagara River, not far upstream from the great waterfall. The river was alive with fish, the fields swelled with corn, and the meadows were covered with sweet berries. For as long as Lelawala could remember, life had been good.

But then one summer sickness came, and many people died. The wife of the chief, Lelawala's mother, was one of them.

The people were worried. "Perhaps the thunder god, Hinu, is angry with us," they said.

Hinu was a mighty being who lived in a cave behind the great falls. He made rain and thunder, but he also protected the people and killed huge underwater snakes that threatened them.

"We must make peace with Hinu," the elders advised. "Perhaps he will lift the curse from us."

So, the people loaded canoes with gifts of food and flowers and sent them down the river, over the falls. Still, day after day, the sickness took young and old alike.

One evening, the medicine man went to the chief. "Hinu is not pleased with our gifts. We must send him something more precious, a thing of youth and beauty."

From the night's shadows, Lelawala listened. She thought of her mother and all the people the sickness had taken. She thought of her desperate father and the fear among those who were left. Lelawala made a decision.

The next morning, Lelawala dressed in her finest clothes and went to her father. "I heard you talking last night. Maybe I can save our people," she said. "I will go down the river to Hinu. I am not afraid."

Her father was stunned. No words came to his lips.

"You must let me go," pleaded Lelawala.

For the last time, she embraced her father. Then she climbed into her canoe. Without another look back, Lelawala set off down the river.

READ LIKE A WRITER

What words and phrases does the author use to help readers follow the sequence of events?

The canoe moved slowly at first, but gained speed as the current grew stronger. In the distance, clouds of smoky mist rose, making the water look like it was on fire. In moments Lelawala would be carried over the falls and swallowed by the river.

The thunder from the falls sounded like thousands of deer pounding the ground. Lelawala was enveloped by moist clouds of spray. Deafened by the roar and blinded by the water, she was thrown from the canoe and tossed over the edge, as if she weighed no more than a feather.

Down, down, down she fell into the boiling waters below. Yet there was no panic or even fear in her. Lelawala felt peaceful and safe, almost like she was being carried in someone's gentle arms.

When the water cleared from Lelawala's eyes, she saw that she was inside a cave. A figure knelt beside her. "I am the son of Hinu," he said. "Stay and take me for your husband."

"I will only stay if you tell me why your father will not help my people," replied Lelawala. "Why is he angry with us?"

"My father is not angry," said the youth. "He is ashamed to let your people know he is not as powerful as they think. There is a monstrous horned snake poisoning the river. This is why your village is dying. The serpent is so enormous, even my father with all of my brothers cannot kill it."

That night, Lelawala thought of her father and appeared in his dream.

"Do not mourn for me, Father," she told him, "for I am safe. Listen, and do as I tell you. I know why our people are sick."

Then she told him about the monstrous snake and how it would appear again.

In two moons' time, the chief and his warriors were waiting by the shore. When the horned serpent rose from the water, they attacked him from their canoes. A fierce battle broke out, and as it did, the sky opened, thunder rolled, and rain poured down.

Bolts of lightning were hurled at the monster. Hinu and his sons had joined the battle. At last, the snake was mortally wounded. The river swept its enormous body toward the falls.

The dying monster got wedged in the boulders at the waterfall's edge. Its head was caught on one side of the river, and its tail on the other. The rocks collapsed under the weight of its writhing body, rearranging the falls into the shape of a bent bow.

That night, the people sang and danced to celebrate the victory. There would be no more sickness. Life, the way they remembered it, could return.

But there were those who were missing from the celebration.

As his people celebrated, the chief slipped away and walked along the riverbank to the falls. There he sat, thinking of those who were gone, and of his daughter in her new life. He listened for her voice in the roar of the water. And he heard it.

Even today, if you happen to stand by Niagara Falls, listen carefully. You just may hear Lelawala and her children calling to each other behind the curtain of water that hides their home.

DIG DEEPER

1. With a group, choose part of the story to read aloud in a Readers' Theatre. Make sure each person has a role.

2. This is a Seneca legend. Tom Hill, a Seneca, worked closely with the author/illustrator to help ensure that the story and drawings were true to that of the Seneca people. Why would this be important?

BOY OF THE DEEPS

BY IAN WALLACE

Where might the "deeps" be?

James's father slung a piece can on the same arm that had carried his lunch for twenty years, then handed a new can to his son. James was no longer a breaker boy, sorting sharp slate from coal with his bare hands. Those days were behind him. This morning he was going underground to work with his father.

"You'll be a good miner, boy," he assured his son. "You have coal in your blood, same as me."

James's mother looked up from the dough that she was kneading. "Take care, my son. You know the deeps is dangerous."

James picked up his water can. He kissed his mother good-bye and slipped out the front door after his father.

Other cottage doors opened and slammed shut behind other men and boys. They walked through the Cape Breton town, huddled together against the salt chill. In the rock beneath their boots ran a coal deposit so rich it was said to stretch for a hundred miles along the coast and out to sea. James had drawn a picture in his head of what that looked like: his father's large hand, black with coal, its fingers splayed as if it were holding up the ocean.

The entrance to the mine jutted out of the earth like a beast rising from the sea. James stopped, holding back. It looks alive, he thought.

READ LIKE A WRITER
How does the author keep your attention?

A seasoned miner whose face was wrinkled with coal dust leaned into him.

"The mine shaft drops a thousand feet, boy," he said. "If you don't fall out of the steel cage, you'll arrive at the place where the Atlantic rests over your head."

He knocked James's hat teasingly off his head and tousled his hair. All the miners laughed except his father. James grabbed his hat and dusted it off.

Inside the lamp cabin they handed in their identification tags and were given their oil lamps.

Then they packed into the steel cage. James could hear his heart beating loud as a drum. At the sound of a bell the cage dropped through the darkness that was blacker than a raven's eye.

With a sudden jolt the cables stopped moving, announcing their arrival. The day shift spilled out into a bustling city underground. Tunnels fanned out like streets in every direction. James took a deep breath. His head was filled with the smell of rock and coal and damp.

The men and boys boarded a rake that rolled down a sloping track. The sound of metal grinding against metal was deafening. Water dripped down from the low ceiling. Finally they reached the stable. Its whitewashed walls shone so brightly that for a moment James imagined the morning sun had followed them underground. The pit ponies snorted and stamped their hooves as if eager to go to work.

James looked up. The Atlantic was above him now. He could hear the layers of rock shifting and creaking, and he was certain that he could hear the ocean, too.

James and his father gathered the tools of their trade, a pick and a shovel each. Then they marched off toward the wall of coal where they would spend the day.

They raised their oil lamps to check for the presence of gases in the mine. James was relieved when their flames did not glow more strongly in the dark but stayed steady. "This room is safe to work in, Da," he said.

His father spit on his bare, calloused hands. Then, wielding the pick, he brought it down. Years of practice were bound up in his swing. All of his weight smashed against the wall. In no time at all he had dug a low trench.

James watched as his father showed him how to bore a hole deep into the wall with an auger. He explained how to pack the hole tight with gunpowder. He showed him how to set the fuses.

James and his father pulled back, turning away as the blast exploded behind them. Great chunks of coal crashed into the trench and spilled out across the ground. A cloud of dust rose so thick that it stung their eyes and gathered in wide circles around their noses and mouths. James coughed hard.

Now they had to collect the coal that had been dislodged from the blast. They swung their shovels as fast as their arms could work.

"Pace yourself, my son," his father cautioned. "We've a long day ahead."

Some of the chunks of coal were the size of James's fist; others he had to lift with both arms. One by one the carts were filled, and ton by ton the pit ponies hauled them away.

When lunchtime came, they sat down for the first time. Only then did James feel the blisters on his hands. Only then did he realize how much his back ached.

He opened his piece can. On top of his bread and cod lay three wild daisies tied with a cherry red ribbon. James laughed with delight and held them up for his father to see.

"That mother of yours is full of surprises," his father said.

James took out his lunch. He set the daisies carefully inside and sprinkled them with water from his can. He would take them home at the end of the day, he decided.

They ate in silence. James was so tired that even chewing was exhausting.

Suddenly his father was nudging him awake. "You drifted off, my son. It's time to go back to work."

James tugged on his father's shirt sleeve. "Look over there, Da!" A rat was nibbling away at the crusts of bread that James had tossed from his lunch. "If that old rat had a shovel for a mouth, he'd be a better miner than you."

His father wrinkled his nose in a ratlike way and twitched his ears. James crossed his eyes and wrinkled his nose, too. In the next moment the rodent was gone. His father fell silent. His ears had caught the sound of the layers of rock overhead, shifting like a pile of stacked plates.

"DA!" James shouted as the soft coal floor swelled beneath his boots and snapping timber cracked like gunfire in his ears.

His father pushed James to the ground, protecting him with his own body. The ceiling was crumbling like a black waterfall, sending up a cloud of dust. James coughed so hard he thought he was spitting coal and blood. In the awful silence that followed James couldn't move. He was pinned to the ground by his father's body.

"DA!" he called out. No reply. "DA!"

James thrust upward with all his strength. He pushed against the weight that was crushing him.

Then suddenly his father's body rolled over onto the ground beside him.

"Da!" he called out. He put his ear to his father's chest. He grabbed him by the shoulders. "We've got to get out of here."

James found his oil lamp and shone it in his father's face. Endless seconds passed before his da's eyes opened. They were as reassuring as the blue sky.

"I'm all right, my son. Just had the wind knocked out of me, is all."

James helped his father to his feet. He lifted his lamp, searching for a way out, but the ceiling's collapse had blocked them in.

James shouted, "Can anybody out there hear me?" No one responded.

He scrambled up the pile of rubble with his shovel and hacked desperately at the slate and coal. His father regained his strength and joined the attack. Sweat ran in rivers beneath their clothes.

James stopped shovelling. He thought he heard the distant echo of metal striking rock. They began to dig harder, faster, stronger, until they had cut a narrow tunnel. A yellow light glimmered in the distance.

"Can anybody hear me?" James shouted.

"We hear you, boy," came a faint reply. "We hear you!"

James clamped his oil lamp in his teeth and began to crawl. The slate and coal tore at his hands and scraped across his shoulders. When he reached the far side, the miners passed him around like a prize puppy.

Soon his father crawled through the opening, clinking and clanging. He had fastened their piece and water cans to the bib of his coveralls.

"You look like a tinker come to sell his wares, Da." All the miners laughed as his father clamped an arm around James's shoulder.

"We'll be enjoying your mother's hearty supper before the sun goes down," said his father. "You've earned it." He handed his son his piece can. James looked inside at the daisies. They were still fresh.

They headed toward the steel cage, the light, and home. Tomorrow they would go down into the deeps again, for they were miners and that was their job.

MEDIA WATCH

Check in newspapers, magazines, and on television for any news about mining today. Make a bulletin board display.

DIG DEEPER

1. Make a story map showing the setting, characters, and events of the story.
2. Safety is a concern in the mines. Research to find out how people have tried to make mining less dangerous.

Setting	Main Characters
Beginning	
Events	

Connect and Share

You've learned about many amazing places in Canada that people can visit.

Now it's your turn to share an amazing place by making a television commercial with a partner.

Choose a place!

- Choose a favourite place in your community.
- Tell someone about it.
- Ask for ideas for your commercial.

Create the commercial!

- Plan an interesting script:
  - Start with something "catchy."
  - Add interesting details.
  - End with an invitation to visit.
- Decide how and when to include props, then make the props.
- Present your commercial to your audience.

PLANNING TIPS

- Make an information web.
- Decide who your audience will be.
- Select information to share.
- Think of props to include.

PRESENTING TIPS

- Sound excited about your amazing place.
- Speak loudly and slowly.
- Use the props to make your commercial more interesting.

Spotlight on **Learning**

Collect

- Gather your notebooks, your writing, and other work you did in this unit.

Select

- Choose two pieces of work that show how you achieved the Learning Goals. (The same piece of work can show more than one goal.)

Tell about your choices

- Tell what each piece shows about your learning.

My choices	I want this in my portfolio because...

Talk and reflect

Work with a partner.

- Together, read the Learning Goals on page 120.
- Talk about how well you met these goals.
- Look through your work for evidence.

Reflect

- What have you learned about gathering and presenting information on social studies topics?
- What have you discovered about amazing places?

Acknowledgements

Permission to reprint copyrighted material is gratefully acknowledged. Every effort has been made to trace ownership of all copyrighted material and to secure permission from copyright holders. In the event of any questions arising as to the use of any material, we will be pleased to make the necessary corrections in future printings.

Student Book

Photographs

2–3 Charles Thatcher/Getty Images; **iv t, 4** Royalty Free/Masterfile; **4–5** CP/Aaron Harris; **5** Royalty Free/Masterfile; **7** AFP/Odd Andersen/Getty Images; **8 clockwise from l** ctv.ca, Comstock/Jupiterimages, Cover of *Kidsworld* Magazine courtesy of MIR Communications Inc., CBC logo used with permission of CBC Radio-Canada; **10** © Jostens Photography; **11 (both)** Amanjeet Chauhan; **12** Mountain West Studios; **13** © 2006 Robert Popkin Photography; **14** © Jostens Photography; **iv b & 15 (both)** Alberta Community Development, Royal Tyrrell Museum; **16 tl** Creatas/Jupiterimages, **tr & b** Ray Boudreau; **17** Ray Boudreau; **v, 18** © OnRequest Images, Inc./Alamy; **18–19** Todd Bigelow/Aurora/Getty Images; **19** Copyright © 1996-2006, The Wright Life; **20 t** Paul Hurt/www.pope.smugmug.com, **middle l** Paul Hurt/www.pope.smugmug.com, **middle r** Juha Kankaanpää/WFDF 2004 World Ultimate & Guts Championships, **b l** Juha Kankaanpää/WFDF 2004 World Ultimate & Guts Championships, **b r** Paul Hurt/www.pope.smugmug.com; **21 t** Paul Hurt/www.pope.smugmug.com, **b** Paul Hurt/www.pope.smugmug.com, **sidebar t** © Heather Bartlett/Heather's Fine Photography, **sidebar b** Juha Kankaanpää/WFDF 2004 World Ultimate & Guts Championships; **22** © Aflo Foto Agency/Alamy; **23** Lucas Oleniuk/Toronto Star; **24** Nino Ardizzi/Blind Kids Art; **25 (all)** Nino Ardizzi/Blind Kids Art; **26** Ray Boudreau; **27** Comstock/Jupiterimages; **28** Gary Duschl, www.gumwrapper.com; **29 t** John Rietveld, www.signalfan.com, **b** Drew Gardner Photographer; **30 t** Marcel Blonk, **b** RoadsideAmerica.com; **31** Alan Weintraub/arcade.co.uk; **42–43** Tony Craddock/Getty Images; **44** Comstock/Jupiterimages; **45 tl** PhotoObjects/Jupiterimages, **clockwise from middle (all)** Ray Boudreau; **46 (both)** Ray Boudreau; **60** Ray Boudreau; **61** Ray Boudreau; **62–63** Philip Lee Harvey/Getty Images; **68** Comstock/Jupiterimages; **69** Creatas/Jupiterimages; **76 (both)** Ray Boudreau; **77** Ray Boudreau; **90** Steve Simon/Klixpix; **91** Steve Simon/Klixpix; **92 (all)** Steve Simon/Klixpix; **93 tl** PhotoObjects/Jupiterimages, **bl** Digital Vision/Getty Images, **tr and br** Comstock/Jupiterimages; **94 clockwise from tl** Comstock/Jupiterimages, Comstock/Jupiterimages, Photodisc/Getty Images **(and vii)**, PhotoObjects/Jupiterimages, Comstock/Jupiterimages; **95 clockwise from tr** PhotoObjects/Jupiterimages, Comstock/Jupiterimages, Comstock/Jupiterimages; **98 (all)** Ray Boudreau; **99** Ray Boudreau; **101** Ray Boudreau; **103** Ray Boudreau; **104** Ray Boudreau; **106** Lawrence Migdale/Getty Images; **107** Ray Boudreau; **108–117 pizza folios** Brand X/Jupiterimages; **118** PhotoObjects/Jupiterimages; **119** Thinkstock/Jupiterimages; **120–121** Ablestock/Jupiterimages; **126 l to r** Cover of "Welcome to Vegreville" brochure: Courtesy of the Vegreville and

District Chamber of Commerce, Cover of *Wow Canada!*: Used by permission of Maple Tree Press, Cover of "Outdoor Adventure in Newfoundland and Labrador" brochure: Image courtesy of Newfoundland and Labrador Tourism, BC Parks: Copyright © Province of British Columbia. All rights reserved. Reprinted with permission of the Province of British Columbia. www.ipp.gov.bc.ca; **127** © Gabe Palmer/Alamy; **128** © Parks Canada/Pagé, D.; **129 t** © Parks Canada/Last, V., **b** © Parks Canada/Butterill, J.; **130 t** chessea.com, **b** chessea.com; **131** chessea.com; **132** Al Harvey/www.slidefarm.com; **viii, 133 t** © Daniel J. Cox/CORBIS, **b** Al Harvey/www.slidefarm.com; **134 (both)** Ray Boudreau; **135** Ray Boudreau; **136–137 background** GOODSHOOT/Jupiterimages; **136** Photo credit: Brian Rodda; **137** Photo credit: Brian Rodda; **138–139 background** GOODSHOOT/Jupiterimages; **138 t** © BMP Stock, **b (and ix t)** Photo credit: Brian Rodda; **139** Al Harvey/www.slidefarm.com; **140** © Tom Bean/CORBIS; **141** Photos.com/ Jupiterimages; **142 t** © Steven J. Kazlowski/Alamy, **b** © John Schwieder/Alamy; **143** © Paul A. Souders/CORBIS; **144–145** Ray Boudreau; **145** Comstock/Jupiterimages; **152** Toronto Star/Firstlight; **154** PhotoObjects/Jupiterimages; **155 t** D Maddock Parsons, **b** Martin Lender; **156 t** Photocanada.com, **middle** Comstock/Jupiterimages, **middle inset** PhotoObjects/Jupiterimages, **bl** CP/Andrew Vaughan, **br** © 1999 Province of PEI; **157 t** © Hemis/Alamy, **bl** Comstock/Jupiterimages, **br** © Paul A. Souders/CORBIS; **158 tl** Comstock/Jupiterimages, **tl inset** Town of Biggar, **tr** Village of Glenboro, **b (and ix b)** © Darlene Lonseth; **159 t to b** Photo by St Paul & District Chamber of Commerce, Ablestock/Jupiterimages, Comstock/Jupiterimages, Russ Heinl/maxximages.com; **160 t** Pat Reece/yukoninfo.com, **bl** Ablestock/Jupiterimages, **br** © Gary Cook/Alamy; **161 l** © Carl & Ann Purcell/CORBIS, **r** DMcLarty_Rankin Inlet NU; **181** Thinkstock/ Jupiterimages

Illustrations

6 Sarah S. Brannen; **32–36** Dave Whamond/Three in a Box Inc; **v, 37–39** Dave Whamond/ Three in a Box Inc; **v, 47, 49–51, 53–54** © Joe Chang; **v, 56–59** © Boshkung Inc.; **vi, 64–67** © Paul O. Zelinsky; **68 l** Archie Comic Publications, Inc., **r** © Lauren Child; **vi, 70–75** Leanne Franson; **vii, 78–82** Dave Whamond/Three in a Box Inc; **vii, 83–89** © James Proimos; **95** Photodisc/Getty Images; **96–97** © Patrick McDonnell; **98–105** Ron Dollekamp/Three in a Box Inc; **vii, 108–117** © Herm Auch and Mary Jane Auch; **viii, 122–125** © Bill Slavin and Esperança Melo; **128** Crowle Art Group; **131** Crowle Art Group; **132** Crowle Art Group; **ix, 146–149** Tina Holdcroft; **150–151** Molly Lamb Bobak (Canadian, b.1922) *Skaters on the Rideau*, 1980, oil on canvas. Purchase, 1980, accession # 1980BM22, The Robert McLaughlin Gallery, Oshawa. Photo: Tom Moore Photography; **154** Photodisc/Getty Images; **ix, 162, 164–169** © Veronika Martenova Charles; **ix, 170–175, 177–178** © Ian Wallace

Text

4–7 "What I Did with My Coin Collection" © ETW Corporation (written by Tiger Woods, illustrated by Sarah S. Brannen); **23–25** "Creating Visions for the Sightless" Reprinted with permission—Torstar Syndication Services; **28–31** Adapted from OWL magazine, "Weird Zone: Strange and True Cool Collections," by Maria Birmingham, March 2004 OWL. Used with permission of Bayard Presse Canada Inc., "Daffy for Ducks!" © 2006 Guinness World Records Limited, a HIT Entertainment Limited Company; **32–36** "What Do Canadian Kids Like to Do?" adapted from *Kids' Take on Media* by the Canadian Teachers' Federation; **37–39** © 2006 Guinness World Records Limited, a HIT Entertainment Limited Company; **40–41** "Skateboard" from *Technically, It's Not My Fault: Concrete Poems* by John Grandits. Reprinted by permission of Houghton Mifflin

Posters

Photographs

Illustrations